AF425150

# THE SECRET *life of* CAREER COACHING

## FIND THE WORK YOU'RE MEANT TO DO BY HELPING OTHERS DO THE SAME

Cara Heilmann

"To be a career coach, one must not only understand themselves but also have insight into what others are searching for in their lives. Through humor and incredible insights, Cara guides us on a journey of self-inquiry. That is the magic and the power of this book."

> ~ **James R. Doty**, MD, founder and director of the Stanford Center for Compassion and Altruism Research and Education and author of the *New York Times* and international bestseller *Into the Magic Shop: A Neurosurgeon's Quest to Discover the Mysteries of the Brain and the Secrets of the Heart*

"If you're considering career coaching as a profession, this book is a must—but it's relevant for anyone in the business world, especially if you're dissatisfied. As a poet, I've had a truly crazy range of pay-the-bills jobs, and hated every one of them. Cara Heilmann's 'magic' gave me the clarity and courage to finally go into business for myself, and for the first time in my life I'm making a living doing something I love and am good at. Her voice is a breath of fresh air in the chaotic and often mysterious world of job search."

> ~ **Amy Glynn**, poet laureate, college advisor, and award-winning author of *Romance Language*

"Once again, Cara Heilmann shares her powerhouse secrets of career coaching. *The Secret Life of Career Coaching* is the foundation for building your business so that you can successfully fulfill your dreams as a career coach while helping others live the life they're meant to."

~ **Michelle Hoffmann**, relationship specialist and international best-selling author of *Life Worth Living, New Management Blueprint*, and the upcoming *Find Love Now*

"Cara Heilmann's *The Secret Life of Career Coaching* blends honest reflection with practical guidance, offering an essential roadmap for aspiring coaches. She shares her own experiences to help readers avoid common pitfalls, emphasizing the swift path to meaningful impact in the coaching field. This insightful book is a must-read for those considering a coaching career, providing the necessary tools to harness their skills and passion effectively."

~ **Lisa Virtue**, founder of Her Career Studio and author of *Career Mama*

"This is a must-read if you are going for a deeper dive into career coaching. Cara's direct and honest guidance makes this book an easy read—entertaining and very educational!"

~ **Nurys Harrigan-Pedersen**, president of Careers in Nonprofits and author of the best-selling book *Make Your Mark: The Smart Nonprofit Professional's Guide to Career Mapping for Success*

"Cara shares a wonderful blend of strategic, psychological, and practical approaches so career coaches can help their clients and grow their business. But these concepts can also aid less formal advisors, such as mentors and teachers. I can't wait to use Cara's concepts to help my students!"

~ **Michael Kennedy**, PhD, visiting faculty in engineering technology management, Eastern Kentucky University and co-author of *Superior Product Development: Managing the Process for Innovative Products*

"A business-rich book—wonderfully crafted with an engaging journey, this book is life-transforming for the entrepreneur and their client. This integration of real-world stories and tried-and-true business foundation deserves to be widely shared throughout the entrepreneurial world. A must-read whether you're a new career coach, or in need of a practice fix."

~ **Aicha Bascaro**, founder and CEO of the American Franchise Academy and author of the best-selling *The Franchise Fix* and *Multi-Unit Franchise Mastery*

"In *The Secret Life of Career Coaching*, Cara Heilmann shares her expertise from decades of work in HR, career coaching, and training career coaches. This book gives foundational knowledge and does not hold anything back for anyone interested in becoming a career coach or even for someone just destabilized by termination, layoff, or a toxic work environment. Cara's perfect record of helping people find their passions and pursue them gives her unique insight into not only how to find work you love but also help others do the same. While, as Cara describes, it is easy to get distracted by life and obligations, this book is full of practical tools to point yourself in the direction of a fulfilling career and help others do the same!"

~ **Meredith Holley**, communication coach, workplace conflict mediator, attorney, and author of the best-selling *Career Defense 101: How to Stop Sexual Harassment Without Quitting Your Job* and *The Inclusive Leader's Guide to Healthy Workplace Culture*

*For my boss who fired my butt: thank you.*
*Without you, I'd still be miserable.*

*For the many coaches I've trained over the years: I'm grateful*
*for our work together to banish bad work days. Forever.*

# TABLE OF CONTENTS

There's a familiar door in front of me. It's not a physical door—there's no hinge, no handle—but I can feel it with something beyond my five senses. I know without even seeing it that it's a door that leads to owning my own business. A path from my current work to something new.

I've always been able to sense doors, those energetic passages between what is and what's next. Some of them have been teeny, tiny buggers, and some have been monstrous. I know this particular door deep in my soul; it's a spiritual one. This door has been waiting for me to walk through it for some time.

I look with my mind's eye, and I see my reflection staring back at me from the door's glass. I've been waffling over whether or not to take the plunge as an entrepreneur, and my reflection looks seriously annoyed. I recently caved and went back to the dark side of working for someone else.

I also see my own fear. Can I do this? What if it doesn't work out? Can I change my mind? Will I be able to come back?

I wish I could see what's beyond my own reflection and feel sure of what will happen. But what I do know is that if I walk through that door, I know I will never come back to this side of it. I can say goodbye to this unhappy place of trying to fit inside other peoples' boxes and shrinking my being to pass through their narrow doorways.

Once I'm on the other side of that door, my life will never be the same. I'm good with that.

# CHAPTER ONE

# Putting the Fun in Dysfunction

Bad things, they say, come in threes. On this day I tick through the whole trifecta before I even sit down at my desk.

The first bad thing is an unwelcome glitch in my morning commute, a drive so routine and reflexive that I can do it on autopilot. Today I somehow coast right past my turn, which means making a slow, three-block detour of Oakland's heavily trafficked one-way streets. Finally, I'm back in front of the landmarks that mark my turn: a brick building covered in graffiti and a run-down Victorian I keep hoping someone will restore to its former glory. How did I miss them?

The second bad thing: the parking card that lets me into the garage of my sixteen-story office building malfunctions—and there's a car behind me waiting impatiently because of course there is. I can feel the unseen driver seething as I press the red button next to the gate, and a voice emanates from the speaker: "How can I help you?"

"Hey, George, it's me, Cara. My card isn't working again."

The gate arm moves as my buddy George lets me in. I remind myself to bring him cookies at lunch.

I make it as far as the elevator when the third bad thing hits. I work on the top floor, the elevator is jam-packed, and thirteen of the elevator's sixteen floor buttons are already lit. I wonder how long I can hold my breath. As I step into the elevator I take a quick gulp of air, and if it weren't for the fact that I don't pass out, I would swear it takes me ten minutes to get to my floor. I burst out of the elevator with a ragged, explosive exhale.

"Good morning, Cara!" says my assistant Lara in a sweet singsong. "Is it another fake it 'til you make it day?"

This is our running joke. Lara knows I'm not happy here. I'm not sure anyone is happy here. Even Lara's best friend, who sits right next to her and got Lara her job, isn't happy. I know this because a) Lara told me and b) you can honestly tell by her face. It's sour, sad, and all too common around here. As Lara once said, "Hey, at least we put the fun in dysfunction."

But the three bad things have already happened, and I feel safe being optimistic. "It's going to be a great day!" I say to Lara as I walk into my office. "What else could go wrong?"

I may be ambivalent about the workplace vibe, but I wholeheartedly love my office. It's on the top floor and right next to the CEO's inner sanctum. I can see down into the chairman's personal gym. And my view is outrageously amazing:

one entire wall is floor-to-ceiling glass through which I often gaze at Lake Merritt's sparkling waters.

I love that I can see if traffic starts on the 24 and skedaddle before it gets bad. I love that I have a comfy chair for my guests when they come to visit. I love that I have a sit-stand desk our ergonomic consultant recommended management buy because she loves me and said she'd do whatever she can to keep me healthy. I close my door and boot up my computer. I've got a project I need to send stat.

The morning flies by. Later, coming back from lunch, I pick up three, warm, softball-sized chocolate chip cookies for George. He thanks me as he holds out my reprogrammed parking card. "Don't hold it near your phone!" he scolds.

George loves me because, as he once told me, I'm the only one around here who knows and uses his name. I love George right back. He's saved my butt on reprogramming fees because the parking card is just lame.

The returning-from-lunch crowd is lighter, and I can breathe on my way back up to the sixteenth floor. My day is turning around, I exult. But I'm wrong. As soon as I step off the elevator, I can tell something is seriously awry.

I get these hits about things, about people. Call it instinct; call it magic—it's been a huge asset in my human resources career. This one doesn't feel like anything good. The entire office looks bleached of color, like I'm watching an old black-and-white film, and the normal sounds are as muted as if I were wearing earmuffs. I look left at the row of assistants busy chatting, working, doing the things they do. They don't seem to be alarmed or sense anything wrong. At the end of the aisle, Lara waves at me and holds out her hand for the cookie I promised I'd bring her.

I take a step toward her, but something prickles, and I slowly swing my head to the right. That's when I see her, our new general counsel, standing three doors down in the doorway of her office. She's looking straight at me.

The last time I experienced this muted, black-and-white Spidey sense was nine months ago. One of our top executives had allegedly been having an affair with another, and somehow the story came out. The exec in question called my boss at eleven at night and, from what I'd been able to gather, issued a sort of half-confession/half-demand. A colleague ended up driving to the exec's apartment where, fueled by alcohol and anger, things got ugly.

Back then, when I walked into the office the next morning, I knew immediately something had gone down. Everything looked just like it does today: the entire floor swam in front of me with a muted, color-drained density that felt like being underwater. I had never wanted to leave more than I did in that moment. I found myself sitting in my boss's office and looking at his black-and-white face as he asked, "Cara, can you make this go away?"

In HR-speak that means "fire them fast and don't let it come back to me, okay?"

Now here I am, staring at the black-and-white face of our new general counsel. I hired her myself and relocated her from another state. She used my realtor to find her new home in my neighborhood. She regards me impassively without expression and I know, deep in my soul, that today it's my rear that's on the line.

Few bosses love it when their human resources leader (that would be me) communicates just how badly things are going with staff, and my boss is no exception. "What about more communication?" I'd suggest. What about walking the halls once in a while saying hello? What about sending little cards of thanks to staff who've DONE amazing work? It appears that my boss has tired of my what-abouts and asked our general counsel to *make it go away*. For the first time in my long career, I am Let Go.

Well. Sort of. Officially I'm "seeking other opportunities," with twelve months of severance to guarantee I'll go quietly. If you think that twelve months of severance for two and a half years of tenure sounds like a lot, keep in mind that I do know where many of the bodies were buried. Damn. I buried some of them myself.

It's not that I'm unable to control my exit that burns the most. It's that I'm being fired for the very thing I was hired to do. "We want trendsetters and free thinkers," my then-future boss had told me during my interview for the job. "I want to be told when I'm doing something that's not in the best interest of the company, what do you think about that?"

As his potential head of human resources, I thought that sounded like a growth mindset executive and a start to an exciting partnership. Many if not most leaders don't really want to know the bad news.

"How do you want to be told?" I asked during my interview.

He liked that answer. And I'd known that it was at that moment that he decided to hire me.

Now it's two and a half years later, and he's tired of being told his ship is leaderless. And so I pack my bankers box full of my stuff and walk away from my amazing office with its amazing view. Before I leave, I glance back and spy my parking card with chocolate chip smudges on it sitting on my desk.

I step into an elevator that still smells of stale food from lunch, balance my box of stuff on a side railing, and face front, silently descending sixteen floors. I wonder if I'll ever ride this elevator again. The car doesn't stop on any other floors, but it seems to take a long time to reach the ground.

I start feeling a little better as I head toward the lobby doors. I pause for a deep, cleansing breath before I walk outside, where the sunlit sky is vivid blue. It seems clearer and brighter than I've ever noticed. And the graffiti is bright neon yellow. Was it always?

I wave to George as I leave the parking garage. Will he notice when I don't return? As I take the exit ramp and point my car down Highway 24, I am overcome with an overwhelming sense of sadness mixed with a huge amount of something that feels new and oddly refreshing.

It takes me a moment to realize that what I'm feeling is relief.

Once I get home, I change into comfy clothes and lounge on the sofa with my dog Muggles, who's ecstatic that I'm here in the middle of the day. As I absent-mindedly scratch her ears, I sense an opening, another door. I hear the click of the knob, and as I turn toward the sound, I feel the pressure of the room escape through the small sliver of an opening that forms. It's like a pressure valve releases, and I give a grateful sigh.

What I see appears to be an iconic, corporate-America double door in front of me, slowly opening in invitation. I can't see what's beyond, but somehow I'm comforted by that. Not being able to see past the threshold feels like a sign that I will somehow create whatever lies ahead. It feels good.

I get up and unpack my bankers box of trinkets, oddly hopeful that something new is right around the corner.

*    *    *

One of the first people I tell about my untimely layoff is my coach, Mary. Mary came highly recommended by a dear friend and colleague at the company that just kicked me out. Mary is her coach, too, because my colleague doesn't think it's fun working in dysfunction. She is one of the most brilliant minds in my field, and after listening to my stories said, "Call Mary." Mary, it turned out, was a seasoned healthcare leader who'd become a life coach back before anyone knew what one was.

I fell in love with Mary during the first conversation I had with her. And it is Mary who now listens to me processing my exit and wondering what I'm meant to do in this world and asks, "Have you thought of starting your own business?"

I feel the oddest little ping.

My mom was a Korean immigrant who scraped her way into the American dream when she married an abusive US serviceman twice her age. She hid from him with the help of the Korean community in Honolulu, which is where she was living when she learned he died of natural causes while working on a US base in Japan. A few years later, my mom married my dad, a local boy from Kauai. She had almost no experience in business, but she could sew. Starting with just a few sewing machines in our home, she managed to create a thriving business in the bowels of Pearl City, Hawaii.

Talking with Mary, I wonder if this is more than just a point of curiosity from my personal history. If somehow entrepreneurship is part of my DNA. Mary's question sets off a vibration in me that rings true. She seems to sense that I need to leave the grind, the constant pressure to perform and conform in a way that isn't quite aligned with my soul. How?

I've worked hard to hide the incongruence between my work and my being. Or at least I think I have. I am a child of immigrants. And even though my mom was a business owner, I wasn't exposed to how the corporate game is played. I didn't have anyone to tell me how I needed to behave to make it at this level.

Despite this I somehow ended up at one of the top business schools in the nation and graduated with decent enough grades to stake my claim in the business world. Picture a small woman from Hawaii running, hair unbound, toward a vast swath of fertile green land and pounding a stake into the ground—manifest destiny!

But now, standing in line at the bank to deposit my severance check, I know that I am more a product of my parents than the roots I formed at my Ivy-ish MBA school. Perhaps, like my mother, I am meant to make something of nothing. Perhaps I am meant to set out on my own.

So I do what so many MBA grads eventually do: I make that chunk of hush money stretch for eighteen months as I fulfill what I feel Mom planted in my DNA long ago. I begin to build a career coaching business, step by step. Certifications earned. Bank accounts opened. Business coaches hired. I'm on my way to creating a business that could make a major difference in the world!

Then disaster hits. I get an offer, and it's a juicy one. Chief Talent Officer for a startup led by a well-known, seasoned pro in her field. The salary is thirty percent more than the HR job from which I was "let go." She's charismatic! She has a plan! She loves my background!

Alas, I go for it.

At first, it's exciting. We're working out of her posh home in Alamo, where we're happily busy brainstorming, ideating, building—all the stuff that startups do. My new boss sits down next to me in her granite kitchen, and we hatch a business that will turn healthcare on its ear.

I'm totally sucked in at this point. I show up each day in my jeans with freshly tinted hair. I feed her dogs and tell them how much I love them. I listen to her ideas for hours. I sit beside her pool, and we elaborate upon her dream of disrupting healthcare. We are poised on the precipice of greatness. The sun is shining on our happy, hopeful, startup faces!

Then one day I sense it, just out of view. Each day, it crawls slowly toward me until the day that I can see it: a shadow at the corner of my vision. My heart sinks with the inevitability of it, and I watch it advance until it's almost touching me. I'm sitting in my boss's office printing something when I feel it.

Dread.

Oh, oh, I know this feeling. It's my life's compass fighting to turn in a different direction. Clouds obscure the sunlight that's been pouring through my boss's glass French doors. The house is covered in the shadows, as if dusk came early. It's my soul crying, "No."

Not only do I know this feeling but I also know why I feel it. Because I did it again; I accepted the easy way. The long, wide road of working a job that isn't my calling, in support of someone else's dream instead of my own. I hate that feeling of discontent. Discord. Misalignment. It's in my mouth—a sharp taste of wrong.

That's when I see something else, deep in my soul. I see the door. That double door of opportunity that slowly begins to unlatch and widen. The pressure in the room releases. It's the same door I saw when I left that corporate job, but it's not opening to let me in—it's opening to let me *out*. This time, instead of seeing what I expected—a sleek lobby, a bank of elevators that lead to a corporate office—I see a path forward.

Smooth brown steppingstones lead me to peer around the frame of the door to what lies beyond. There, I see a glimpse of verdant grasses and vibrant flowers, buoyant white clouds and blue, blue skies.

I turn in my resignation the next day. And then I go back to building the business I am meant to.

*    *    *

On paper, I am an executive career coach who trains and certifies others to do the same. But I know—and you will discover—that what I do is nothing less than magic. And you don't have to consider yourself a magician to do the same.

If you're reading this book, you've already been through a few doors yourself. Many of them may have been a bad fit.

Perhaps some closed just a little too sharply behind you. But this door is different. It leads to a career coaching business that will use all of you, in the best possible way. A business in which you will make a solid difference in the world, grow and thrive, and enjoy all the rewards that come with a life well-lived.

I'm going to teach you the foundations of building your business so you don't ever have to wonder if you can do it or if you can make it ever again. Let me pave the path for you so that you can live the life you're meant to.

Ready?

# CHAPTER TWO

# If I'm a Professional, Why Am I So Scared?

I'm a few years into a booming career coaching business. I applied my MBA smarts and my DNA blood. I'm chugging along helping people land amazing jobs. I did it. I'm invited to help a company that's shutting its doors after forty years, and I'm onsite teaching their recruiting team (who they didn't lay off in hopes of helping their beloved employees land on their feet) to become outplacement consultants.

It feels freaking incredible.

It feels even more amazing when three different life coaches ask me to help them.

Newly certified as coaches, they all want to make a difference. But somehow being a life coach isn't snagging clients. "Can you teach me what you're doing?" they ask. One confesses that helping someone get a new job is more satisfying—and lucrative—than simply saying, "I can help you with your life transitions!" and hoping the client can figure out what that means.

In response, I begin to create an outline of what I do that allows me to be extremely happy and successful in helping professionals land their dream jobs. Then I build a curriculum that fills the gaps. Like water flowing from top to bottom, I show these three how to create a career coaching practice that meets their needs—everything they love about being a life coach—and helps them create something meaningful, lasting, and profitable.

The resulting course is solid. It's about being a great—not just good—career coach. I pour all I know and have into this curriculum. It is twenty-plus years of insight and experience, combined with all I've done as an entrepreneur to grow and scale a sustainable career coaching practice. And a sprinkling of magic.

That's what you're going to find in the pages of this book. Part instruction, part woo-woo.

I didn't get where I am all by myself. I see the divine thread of love and possibility that has sustained me and led me throughout the years to create what I have in order for all of us to build a better world. One of happiness. Fulfillment. An expression of all our talents so that we can live out our life's mission on Earth. It's nothing less than magic.

That magic is a cord. And it weaves through these pages of deep experience so that you, too, can build something remarkable. Something that not only lifts you up but also raises up everyone who works with you.

Not sure if career coaching is for you? Let me share a little about three different people I've trained—and their journeys—so you can feel confident in your heart of hearts that I can help you build the company of your dreams.

These three people are from different parts of the world, and they are all career coaches I've mentored. They each came to me with the same look of excitement and fear. Can they really do this? Can they never set foot and sit their bums down in a cube again? Never have to work with a boss who is cruel or dismissive or blind to their talents? These three coaches all started out feeling like you are right now: excited and anxious. Is this too good to be true?

Nancy is an Agile coach who finally has it out with her boss, a total butthole who constantly belittles her in front of her own teammates and sometimes even clients. Pushed to her limit, she quits over text, calling her boss a few choice words in the process. Afterward, she Zooms me in a dark moment of self-doubt and despair.

I ask what I've been wondering since our most recent call: "Would you want to become a career coach?"

The storm clouds part, and her eyes meet mine with fear but also no small amount of anticipation and excitement. "Do you think I would make a good career coach?"

I do.

Today, Nancy has an Enterprise with a capital E. She's a solopreneur bringing in close to $300,000 USD a year with a career coaching business that touches the lives of hundreds of people in Canada and beyond.

Jenny is a life coach whose practice isn't coming together as she hoped it would. She sees a Facebook post of mine asking if any life coaches out there are considering becoming career coaches. She studies with me and gets the certification, but she decides to try to build her business on her own. When that doesn't work, she signs with outplacement behemoth Lee Hecht Harrison and ends up in massive debt—twenty grand in the hole!—eleven months after graduating.

She reaches out to me and asks if I'll bring her into what I call the Path: twelve months of business support following training and certification. Three months in, she hits $8000 in monthly revenue and starts paying off her credit card debts.

And then there's Geri. She has twenty years of HR and recruiting experience under her belt and is newly certified as a career coach, but she still lacks confidence that she can stop selling trinkets on eBay and turn career coaching into a real business. She's just now getting into the swing of it, and I can see the future that awaits her unless she changes her negative mindset. One hampered by overthinking, self-condemnation, and an ongoing internal self-prosecution detailing her alleged flaws, her doubts, and her past missteps. By her own admission, she limits herself, despite the fact that every single person who knows Geri says that she's remarkable. I wonder what could happen if she ever realizes what a force of nature she is.

Let me be clear: I'm only a few steps ahead of Nancy, Jenny, and Geri. And my mentors, at least some of them, were just a few steps ahead of me. Some of them were business leaders who'd achieved more reach and financial success than I could right out of the gate. But they weren't career coaches, so I had to convert their teachings and advice into a career coaching business model. Nothing I learned was plug and play. This won't be the case for you.

In the upcoming chapters, I tell you what I kept, what I modified, and what worked for me and for over 130 other career coaches I've trained at the time of this writing. I share my lessons because I fell down hard, and I have a lot of scars on my knees. And because deep down inside I know this is what I am meant to do in this world, to give hope to those who feel like it's just too hard and to make it simple. Not because you can't understand its complexity but instead so that you can look at it from a different perspective.

I'll tell you all that I recommend. What to do differently than I did: differently from how I tried to start my business and from how I've worked in corporate America. I'll break things down so that you can see the long horizon, a concept I learned from a neuroscientist. When we know where we're going in the long run, who we are to become on the long horizon, the struggles we face each day go by in a flash. Like a flare in the sky or a flame extinguished, the stuff that feels so hard today is fleeting. And those challenges are both unavoidable and necessary for our own journey to be the fullest expression of ourselves.

Because that's what we're talking about, finally. The fullest expression of ourselves. Yours, and your clients. For the first time in my life, after twenty years of C-suite, post-MBA, post-climbing the ladder, I am finally doing something that uses all of me. And that is incredibly fulfilling.

That's why I chose to share all my secrets in the next few chapters. The nuts and bolts of being a career coach, so that you can avoid a few bandaged knees and get to helping people faster than I did. It will seem to you sometimes that I'm someone who has it all together, who is much further down the path. I invite you, as you take this step forward, to pause for a moment and look behind you. Because there are other sisters and brothers who may be looking to you to show them the way.

You may find it heartening that much of this process builds on what you already know. So that you can do what you know deep down in your heart, in your soul, that you were meant to do: help others. Like these three women. I want you to feel encouraged and to know that you can do it. Life is too short to do something that uses only half of who you are.

My hope is that you, like me, will learn what it is to live fully expressed, right to the edge of your skin. Not only as a career coach but also as a healer and teacher. This is powerful and genuine magic, not just a parlor trick like pulling a rabbit out of a hat. And it all starts right here.

# CHAPTER THREE

# Oh, the Places You'll Go

Career coaching isn't Kelly Services, and I'm not teaching you to start a temp agency.

I say this because career coaches sometimes get confused questions from random people at dinner parties. "So you help people get, like, gigs?" Or "Oh, yeah, I have a friend who saw a career person to find out if she typed fast enough to be a personal assistant."

You will not be placing applicants in temporary positions. Instead you'll be using your own personal life experience, your training, and your expertise to help professionals figure out what's next and where they fit in the world. You are doing nothing less than guiding others to find their purpose, their Why.

It's a pretty big deal.

You won't just be reviewing résumés and listening to your clients recite a laundry list of wants. You'll be reading between the lines and using everything you've learned and know to hear the cry of their souls. That includes your intuition. You'll find yourself suddenly knowing something in a flash of insight that you didn't know you knew. You'll hear a whispered word or phrase that no one actually said out loud. You'll see, with conviction and clarity, what your client needs and how to successfully coach them on their career trajectory.

I know this because that's the way it works for me as well as the many other career coaches I've trained.

You don't have to be clairvoyant in order to do this. All that's required is being a student of human nature (which you are simply by paying attention and being alive) and an active listener. All you need is to be willing to keep an open mind, open eyes, and open heart. Your clients will be in part blinded by anxiety, fear, agitation, and, for those who've lost a job, grief. You will see clearly for them when they simply can't. You will, I promise, know just what to say and do.

*    *    *

Nearly six feet tall with the physique of a long-distance runner, Laurie Ramsay is a high achiever. She's the vice president of a national running store chain and fifteen years into an impressive career leading multiple retail stores and coaching first-time marathon runners. She has a career placement certification under her belt. She sits in my three-day business launch training class with years of experience that you might think are all she needs to be a successful career coach.

But Laurie says, "I'm lucky I found you" when we go around the room for introductions. "Only now do I feel I know what I need to do to be a career coach. Only now do I feel confident." After ten weeks of integrating the ideas provided in our senior professional career coach certification program, Laurie feels ready to start her own business.

It certainly won't take you ten weeks to read this book unless you're easily distracted or a very deliberate reader. But in the following pages, I'll be taking you through those ten weeks so that you can feel as confident as Laurie now does. This is a clear, simple process that starts at the bottom and builds upon itself. In the end, you'll know exactly how to create a successful career coaching practice.

I'll share the pitfalls so you don't waste time like I did, chasing the other business coaches in different market segments. I'll make sure you can begin coaching people as quickly as possible, so you can make the income you deserve and, more importantly, make a difference in the world as you're meant to do. So that you finally have a job that uses all of you.

We'll start by laying a solid foundation for your business— one that actually starts in your own mind. Using established neuroscientific techniques, you'll be able to clearly envision and thus create your success. I'll work with you to identify your niche—who do you most want to work with?—and develop a client avatar so you know everything you can about them. A startup checklist helps you set up your business quickly, legally, and financially soundly.

Next we pivot from the fundamentals of your business to the foundation of client success. I'll help you get prepared to answer the question so many clients will, at least in some form, ask: "What am I meant to do when I grow up?"

You'll learn how to identify your client's Ideal Job so that you set them off on the right career path. And you'll confront someone you already know and sometimes spend way too much time listening to: the anxious naysayer part of your brain called the amygdala.

We'll cover the mechanics of your coaching practice: helping your clients create a dossier that includes a résumé, cover letter, and LinkedIn profile. You'll learn just what your client needs to give you and how to get it all organized before you begin to write. I'll share the steps that make this intuitive and easy so that you can create client dossiers efficiently, effectively, and powerfully. Your clients will love you for this.

You'll also master the basics of writing a killer résumé that not only captures recruiters' attention but also compels them to want to talk with your client. More interviews mean more choices.

Once the dossier is complete, it's time to create a "go-to-market" strategy for your client. You'll discover the best job sites, how to effectively network, how to leverage external recruiters, and how your client can keep all this organized. Here your client needs a lot of your support because the rubber is meeting the road and anxieties are running high. Most clients feel a good deal of nervousness when facing the job interview.

You'll see, as I do, that a significant factor in your and your client's success is confidence. I'll share the secrets that have helped thousands of the people I've worked with land job offers because of the confidence they've exuded during the interview process. I'll talk about the power of storytelling and how anyone can become more charismatic in ways that grow their potential for executive presence. You'll get a tool that will help you coach your clients to nail their interviews.

Your job isn't over when your client lands the gig. You'll learn how to keep in touch with them over the next ninety days so that when their new boss turns to them and says, "You're the best hire I've ever made," your client will turn to you and think you're the best investment *they've* ever made. You'll learn how I end my coaching calls in a way that closes the circle of coaching and opens my clients' personal doors to individual success.

If all that sounds like a lot, it is. But I promise that it won't be boring. It will be filled with insights. Tips. Magic. Because that's what makes it all worthwhile, when you help someone, once again, remember what a rockstar they are and land a job.

# CHAPTER FOUR

# The Magic of Your Brain

All coaches work from experience. All coaches work with tools. But all coaches—including career coaches—also coach from *ourselves*. Our greatest gifts come from within us: our intuition, our compassion, our curiosity, our determination. One of the most powerful gifts we bring to our coaching is what we've learned from our own struggles. Our highest wisdom often comes from whatever hell we've survived.

There's a big caveat here: that inferno must be firmly in the past and dealt with. We must coach from our healed scars, not our wounds. It's important to coach from a place of clarity rather than from our own unresolved issues or ongoing struggles.

Our coaching begins with us.

When I see a career coach struggling with a client, I know it's almost always because of a blind spot or something the coach herself is troubled by.

Gloria is one of our certified coaches. After she graduates from our course, she's the only International Association of Career Coaches (IACC) coach in her state, which in my opinion gives her a huge advantage. But she's struggling to get her business off the ground. She has just one client, a senior leader in marketing who's negotiating salary with a prospective employer and who's uncomfortable asking for more money.

"It's frustrating," Gloria says. "She knows she's worth more, but she can't seem to find the confidence to ask for it."

The other coaches in Gloria's cohort jump in to help her by suggesting different techniques they've used successfully to help female clients ask for more money. Then it hits me: Gloria is conflicted about her own value as a career coach.

I ask, "Gloria, what do you think is holding her back?"

"So many things," Gloria says. "She's never earned that kind of money. She doesn't want to start off her employment on the wrong foot. She's never asked before and isn't sure how to."

Gloria pauses. Then, as something clicks, she gives me a clear-eyed look. "Oh, I see where you're going," she says. "I struggle with these things in my business too."

Coaching will show you where your own blind spots are every time. That's why my career coach training, like this chapter, begins with mindset.

The first lesson I teach is that we ourselves are the number one limiter of our own success.

It isn't the market. It isn't the demand for our services. It isn't advertising. It's us. So this chapter starts you off with a few magic tricks I've learned to get your thoughts on your side.

I urge you to lean into this because it isn't just the first lesson but also the second and third and last lesson we learn as career coaches. Your own brain limits you. And there are steps you can take to overcome that. Learn how, for yourself and for your future clients.

## ENVISION YOUR SUCCESS: NEUROSCIENCE MEETS GRIT

One of my favorite athletes is Steph Curry of the Golden State Warriors. I find him incredibly joyful to watch on the basketball court, in no small part because of his buzzer-beating three-point buckets from near half-court. When Steph has the ball in his hands, the crowd anticipates they're going to see something amazing, and he usually delivers. In athletics this is called "clutch." It means the player keeps their cool and performs extremely well under very high pressure, even when the entire game is on the line.

In career coaching, we see clutch when our client walks out of a high-stakes job interview knowing they just nailed it. We as coaches experience moments of clutch as well, like when we hit our monthly revenue targets for the first time. They and we know that when it really counts, we come through.

What can we do as coaches to increase the odds of our success—to achieve more clutch instead of crash and burn? This is where neuroscience comes in. Clutch isn't about what you do so much as it's about your mindset when you do it. Learn this concept well, so you can teach it to your clients as they go through the job search process.

You may already know that athletes use visualization as a tool for success. They imagine or visualize a successful play, shot, hit, or run because they know it helps them perform at a higher level. Why? The answer is that our brains can't distinguish between a real and an imagined experience. When an athlete visualizes a successful free throw or broad jump, that visualization stimulates the same parts of the brain that physically performing those actions would. This kind of mental rehearsal conditions the brain for successful outcomes. We can do this as well as career coaches.

Here's the script of a meditation I use in my training to help new career coaches get their brains on board with their own success. You might want to record yourself reading this aloud so you can play it back and relax into it.

I'm going to take you on a short journey. Turn off your devices so you can be undisturbed for the next ten minutes. Sit in a comfortable spot with your feet on the floor or out in front of you. Let your arms fall to your side or rest them on your lap with your palms facing up. Close your eyes. Take a deep breath and relax. Take another deep breath in and feel your body relax. Listen to my voice and imagine. Let your imagination go. Take another deep breath, relax, and imagine. Focus on your breath. Flowing in and out of your body. Replenishing, filling your body with life.

Imagine your life now with your mind's eye. Imagine the people who love you, and the ones you love. Imagine that you are surrounded by those who are part of your love circle. See them standing near you, smiling. See them in your mind. Feel their love and support. See yourself sitting where you are with your love circle around you. Some are touching you. Hands on your shoulders, your head. Connecting you with their love and support. Feel their support.

Now think about your goal to be a certified career coach. Think about this goal and what it means to you. What about it is important to you? What about it will add value to your life? What about it will add to the lives around you? Think about how it will expand your life and enrich those around you, your love circle. Think about it and see your goal in your mind's eye.

Now imagine yourself going forward into the future: one week, two weeks, three weeks. Go forward into the future. It is now one month in the future. You have started on the road to success. What are you doing now? What does it feel like to be on the road to achieving your dream? You are making it happen. You are moving forward. What do you feel? Let that feeling soak in.

Continue going forward. It is now six months in the future. You have completed the certification program and are busy meeting with clients. You are certified and you are seeing the benefits of your efforts. What are you feeling now? What emotions do you feel as you are feeling the benefits of your efforts? Imagine it all.

Now continue going forward. It is now one year in the future. You have fully accomplished your goal. You have built your coaching practice to where you want it to be. You have achieved what you set out to achieve. See yourself. What are you doing? Who are you with? What are people saying to you? And what are you saying to them? Stand there for a moment. See your client's faces, smiling and thanking you. Feel the moment. Knowing you've helped many people. You've made a difference in people's lives. Feel how that feels. Soak that feeling in. See your love circle. See the rich and vibrant connections you have with those in your love circle.

Take a deep breath. Take another deep breath. Relax. Smile. And when you're ready, open your eyes. If you wish, take a moment to write down what you remember. Things that stand out to you. Faces you've seen. Words they've said.

Our brains learn through repetition, so I suggest you take yourself through this exercise regularly. I also recommend adapting this exercise for specific scenarios you might be struggling with like sales calls, webinars, or speeches. Imagine them going well. Imagine your very happy clients as you wrap up your engagement with them.

As you work through this exercise, you may hear from a certain something you've known all of your life. It's been your biggest source of inaction and fear, but at the same time it's possibly saved your life.

Meet your amygdala.

## AMYGDALA: FRIEND OR FOE?

The amygdala is a tiny part of your brain, but it's a very big deal. It's an almond-shaped part of the limbic system adjoining the temporal lobe of the brain, and it's involved in emotions of fear and aggression. You know it as your fight-or-flight response.

Historically our amygdala regularly saved our lives. Back when we were hunting woolly mammoths, it told us when a predator was near and spurred us to run away. When we were young children, it did the same. Instead of our dashing across a busy street, our amygdala piped up and said, "Wait, Mommy said to hold a grown-up's hand."

Your amygdala is a valuable advisor for you even today. When you get that creepy feeling, when the hair rises on the back of your neck as you walk into a situation, when you know something is off, your amygdala raises the alarm. It says, "Whoa, this is dangerous. Get ready to run or defend yourself."

The problem is that your amygdala lacks discernment. It can't tell you which situations are life-threatening, and which are exciting new ventures. All your amygdala knows, whether you're walking down a dark alley or considering a new career, is that there's risk. Your amygdala's job is to keep you safe. But often, especially for those of us lucky enough to live in a relatively safe part of the world, your amygdala ends up keeping you small.

Understand that for our clients, the opportunity to step into something new may hit their amygdala as an unacceptable risk. You can make a big difference here by being the one who helps them identify what's going on in order to calm their amygdala down.

It helps many of my clients to give this part of themselves a name. In fact you may find that some of your clients, even those who've never heard of their amygdala, already have a name for this voice of caution. Negative Nelly. The Devil on My Shoulder. The Reptilian Brain. The Saboteur. If they don't have a name already, helping them come up with one helps them differentiate this risk-avoidant voice from their own.

Depending on your client's background, your client may refer to it and know its voice through their spiritual beliefs. I find it helpful to understand where my client's coming from. I ask them to tell me a little about their spiritual beliefs and background when talking about the amygdala so I can speak about it in their own language.

For example, a client who tells me they grew up in the Catholic church might resonate with the idea of the Devil on My Shoulder. An overly critical voice that judges them and operates in fear. With a client whose beliefs are based in science, I refer to the amygdala as negative self-talk and speak in terms of the limbic system and neuroscience. And for clients who are into New Age beliefs like chakra balancing, spiritual guides, and Abraham-Hicks, I may refer to it as incongruence, being out of alignment with the higher self.

As a career coach working with professionals, I usually go with neuroscience and use the term amygdala to talk to them about the evolutionary function of this part of their brain. As you learn more about who you're working with, their beliefs, and their language, you can modify your vernacular to be more aligned with them.

## Your Amygdala Doesn't Live in the Present

It can't. It's either judging past action/inaction or off in the future predicting disaster. When your amygdala is stuck in the past, it sounds like a lot of woulda-shoulda-coulda. When it's future-casting, it sounds like anxiety and worry about all the terrible things that might happen. When these thoughts cause our clients to spin out, it can really hold them back in the job search process.

It will help you—and your clients—if you can remember that the amygdala gets triggered throughout the job search process. The first time it rears its head is usually when we're identifying the client's Ideal job. This sounds like a terrible risk to the amygdala, and it reacts by wanting at all costs to keep the client safe by being discouraging. It says, "Yeesh, can I really do that job? I'm a bit nervous about that idea."

During the résumé and dossier creation process, the amygdala says stuff like, "I don't have a lot of quantifiable achievements." That's assuming your client's amygdala allows itself to be seen and heard at all. Often it goes into hiding and takes the client with it. You'll know that's what's happened when your client says they haven't completed their homework or struggles to answer your questions.

When your client starts applying for jobs, the amygdala pipes up and says, "If I get this job, I'm not sure I'll like that commute." The client hasn't even received an offer yet and already their amygdala is trying to talk them out of it. Anything to keep them in what it believes to be safety.

During the interview process, the amygdala is loudly screaming in their ear and getting in the way. When they're negotiating, the amygdala says, "I might lose the job offer if I ask for too much money."

The amygdala still keeps yammering even after your client has landed the job. "Shhh," the amygdala says during onboarding. "Don't ask questions, just take notes."

When you hear any of these kinds of statements, it's time to talk to your client about their amygdala in whatever terms they can understand and find relatable.

Just as I might be a few steps ahead of where you are now, you will be a few steps ahead of your clients. You don't have to have it all figured out—and you likely won't—but you'll have some nuggets of experience and wisdom to share with them. It's important to do self-work so that you are clear, calm, and well-positioned to support your clients. The more attuned I am to my own amygdala, for instance, the easier it is for me to hear the fear and panic in others. Then it's easier for me to help them.

Model what you'll teach. Learn to quiet your own amygdala because left unchecked, it can lead you down a path of sleepless nights, anxiety, depression, and worse. And the job search process can be very depressing. Some of your clients may have been out of work for a while and already in a circle of despair. They'll need your steady guidance and encouragement—and what you'll teach them about calming and grounding themselves.

There's a very real way in which we're entering someone's life through the lens of their career. When I first told my Coaches Training Institute colleagues that I was going to be a career coach, I was met with a lot of confused looks. They understood once I'd say that I am a coach entering someone's life wheel through the slice of their career. I'm helping them with something vitally important to them at a time in their lives that can be quite discouraging. I'm making a real difference in their experience and in their lives.

So will you.

When you learn to quiet your amygdala, you can experience a profound sense of peace, joy, and happiness. And you can help your clients do the same.

There are so many resources out there to help people quiet this part of their mind. Here are a few that come to mind:

- Eckhart Tolle, *The Power of Now*
- Don Jose Ruiz, *The Four Agreements*
- Esther Hicks and Abraham-Hicks

- Brooke Castillo's *Self Coaching 101*
- *Thanks for the Feedback* by Stone and Heen
- *Mindset* by Carol S. Dweck

All of these contain wisdom that can help you in your quest to quiet your amygdala. They also have plenty to say about human nature, our evolution as a species, and the importance of mindset in calling to us the experiences we want.

Here's what I do to help my clients tame their amygdala:

1. Recognize its voice;
2. Learn to shut it off;
3. Do the above faster and faster.

Here's how it looks in action. My client Ed makes a mistake at work and brings it up during our conversation. He's really frustrated and beating himself up. Two weeks later when we chat, he gives a heavy sigh. I ask what's up, and he talks about that mistake from two weeks ago. He is still carrying the incident with him.

Another client, David, is really concerned because he's never completed his bachelor's degree, and he feels like it's the biggest thing holding him back. Never mind that he has a terrific job as a technology specialist at a quite famous electric car manufacturing company. The fact that he already has a job in the role he's seeking doesn't dissuade him; he's convinced his lack of a degree is in his way.

Paula tells me that she's never negotiated a job in her life. She feels like she's shortchanged herself all of these years and is a terrible example to her two daughters. I ask her if in her current job, she still feels like she's not being fairly compensated, and she says, "No, but I keep thinking about it."

Ed, David, and Paula have painful, broken-record stories that continue to play in their heads even when those stories have no basis in current fact. Stories like these get in our clients' way. In the way of their achieving career satisfaction even when it's right there within reach.

When I hear stories like these, I know it's the perfect opportunity to talk about the amygdala, its role, and the consequences of allowing it to keep us small. Then I share tips on how they can control it.

## First: Recognize Its Voice

The first step is to recognize its voice. I help clients do this in several ways. I point out when I'm hearing it and see if they can hear it too. I challenge my clients to spend one entire day trying to recognize when it's speaking and to journal what it's saying. I ask my client to be aware of any physical manifestations of the amygdala like clenching their jaw, tapping their finger, twirling their pen, etc. Finally, I ask my client to close their eyes, think about their story, and tell me where they feel it in their bodies. What does it feel like? From these jumping-off points, it's easier for them to recognize when their amygdala is speaking.

## Second: Learn to Shut It Off

Sometimes simply recognizing that distinctive, negative voice is enough for a client to catch it and shut it down. Other times I suggest a mindfulness practice like deep breathing, meditation, prayer, song, worship, exercise, or journaling. Getting quiet and clear calms the amygdala right down.

There are several transformational coaches who teach a version of inquiry: a ritualized form of Q&A that can disempower fear and anxiety. One model, taught by author Byron Katie, goes like this:

Is my painful thought true?

Is it objectively, factually true? Would anyone and everyone agree with this thought?

How do I feel when I think this thought?

Who would I be without this thought?

And finally:

Can I turn this thought around and find the inverse just as true or more true?

What does that tell me about my thoughts? Are they fact, or simply hypotheses?

Another model, taught by coach Brooke Castillo, uses the acronym CTFAR:

Circumstance
Leads to
Thought
Which leads to
Feeling
Which leads to
Action (or inaction)
Which leads to
Results

You can work this in both directions: starting with the painful circumstance, or starting with the results.

For instance:

Circumstance: I get paid $75K a year.

Thought: I'm not getting paid enough.

Feeling: Anger, shame.

Action: Stomp around the office, feel bad, turn in projects past deadline.

Result: I don't get a raise (notice how these results prove the original painful thought).

But if we work it in reverse:

Result: I didn't get a raise in my last review.

Action: I would have had to perform better to get a raise.

Feeling: Hopeful—there's something I can do to affect my salary.

Thought: I will prove to my supervisor that I deserve a raise.

Circumstance: I get a raise.

This model teaches us how to change our feelings by changing our thoughts. It works because it is our thoughts, rather than our circumstances, that drive our results.

**Third: Learn to Do It Faster and Faster**

Practice this yourself about some of the crappy circumstances in your life. It's easier to learn if you start with small stakes, like your kids not picking up their socks and putting them in the hamper, or getting into your car and finding someone has left the radio on really loud.

Once you've learned to manage your amygdala through awareness and better mental hygiene, you can teach your clients how to do it too.

One caveat: you don't want to eliminate the amygdala from doing its job altogether. It can literally save our lives. Instead what you're doing is shortening the time you might spend in spin, unable to discern a true risk from taking a chance on something new. Recognizing the voice sooner means ending the spin sooner.

All great athletes have learned how to do this. So have successful entrepreneurs. So will you.

# CHAPTER FIVE

# The Magic of Your Niche

I know a woman who calls herself the Widow Coach. She's a life coach who coaches women who've lost their partners. Another woman is the Vet Recruiter—she recruits for veterinarian staff positions.

Both these women are very successful at what they do. Their clients have no problem figuring out their areas of expertise. If they simply marketed themselves as generalists—a life coach who works with everybody, or a recruiter who works with all positions in all fields—they definitely would not be as successful.

Your coaching business has a better chance of success if you create a niche.

A lot of people I talk to are confused about niches. It doesn't mean excluding anyone who doesn't fit into a particular box. The Widow Coach doesn't work just with women—she works with men too. But her marketing is targeted 100 percent to women. That's her niche.

When I wrote my first book, *The Art of Finding a Job You Love*, I didn't expect that only people who were miserable at work or out of a job would read it. In fact I got messages from people in all kinds of different career situations who'd bought and read my book. Some needed jobs right away. Some wanted to stay right where they were, but they wanted a deeper connection to their work.

Niches are magnetic. They attract the very people you target—and a lot more of them too.

Consider your niche your stake in the ground. You declare your turf, your area of focus. It's where you'll put your energy and attention, trusting that others will wonder what all the fun's about and want to play too.

Here are a few career coaching niches that I believe would be phenomenal. You could be a career coach for:

- Individuals with disabilities
- Parents returning to the workforce
- The LGBTQIA+ community
- Men over forty
- Latina women in technical careers
- New grads
- People who've had a traumatic work experience
- Introverts

See how very specific these niches are?

"Career coach" is not a niche. It says nothing to your potential clients. Imagine how a restaurant that only advertises that it serves "food" would struggle to attract clientele. When you want to go out to dinner, you decide to go to a burger joint, or a sushi bar, or someplace that specializes in northern Italian dishes or Greek desserts. You go to the restaurant that serves what you want.

When you're looking for a new job, you seek out a career coach who specializes in helping people like you.

Interestingly niching is exactly what we ask our clients to do. The more generic a candidate looks in a job search, the less compelling their dossier is. A client who says, "I can do everything!" will take a very long time to land a job. The more specific they are in their job search, the more attractive they are.

Niching also helps career coaches as business owners. When you know your area of specialty, your advertising, sales calls, and all communications about what you do are much, much easier to put across. This is the power of creating a niche.

This is also an opportunity to integrate your passions, your skills, and your experiences into one compelling package. To bottom line your superpowers and translate them into a business so that your niche not only attracts clients but also fully engages the person integral to that business: you. The niche you create should reflect all that you love about what you do.

Take me for example. I've told you that I'm gifted at helping people find out what they're meant to do. I "just know" when someone is doing what they love. And if they are not, I "just know" what might be a better fit. This gift helped me tremendously when I was a recruiter charged with finding talent. I'd know when someone was the right person for the job, and I knew when the candidate decided to accept my counteroffer. How? I don't know—I've always been like this. When I was a kid, I knew who was calling when the phone rang. I made sure to integrate this gift into my business.

What do you love to do? Speaking? Teaching? One-on-one coaching? Working with groups? Maybe you love writing résumés, or designing LinkedIn profiles. Might you be a master at drawing forth someone's inner goddess?

Take a moment now and consider what your niche might be. Write it down. And then use this checklist to verify that it's a strong enough niche.

- ✓ Is my niche unique?
- ✓ Is my niche searched online?
- ✓ Does my niche have a lot of topics to talk about?
- ✓ Is there a nice sub-niche (a specialized category) within the niche?
- ✓ Are the topics evergreen (always relevant)?
- ✓ Is my niche specific to my gifts?
- ✓ Does the niche represent my authority?

## YOUR CLIENT AVATAR: WHO YOU'RE MAKING MAGIC WITH

Just as you need to know your area of specialty (niche), you also need to identify your client avatar. You may hear this called a customer avatar, your ideal client, a marketing persona, or a customer profile. No matter which term you use, this type of person you most want to work with and who will be most likely to purchase your services. You also want them to become a good source of word-of-mouth marketing as they recommend you to family and friends.

You'll end up coaching all kinds of people. But they'll have one thing in common: they'll be attracted to you specifically because of your niche. Your niche is a starting point to understanding who your ideal customer is, and that, in turn, will help you build a more successful business, create a more on-target brand, and develop more effective marketing.

Since these people are so important to your business success, it's essential to develop a detailed understanding of who they are and what makes them tick. You may need to do some research to understand their demographic and psychographic details so you can define and attract this ideal client easily. There are many different places where you can find information to help you better identify your perfect client, including social media, Google Analytics, competitor research, industry data, and your current customer data.

You might not want to do it all just yet though. It's a pretty deep rabbit hole. One day, when you have more time to spend on your marketing, I recommend you go down it to learn more. For now I want to teach you what will work in the short-term so you can begin to coach people and launch your business as quickly as possible.

Down the road, you may want to check out and invest in a career coach cohort I lead called The Path for Graduates. Its members are all graduates of the IACC, and among other things, they test different marketing techniques and then share what worked and what didn't. This community is an excellent resource for when you're ready to expand your marketing efforts.

By finding out what's already working, you can save a lot of time, money, and hassle.

For now, though, let's keep it simple. You're just starting out, and it makes sense to get up and running quickly. So start your client avatar work by thinking of just one person. And to make it as easy as possible, we'll start with someone you know.

1. Think of one person who is in your niche. A real person. Someone you know, like, and would really like to help. For example if your niche is helping introverted people find jobs, think of someone in your life who's an introvert.
2. Get a photo of your ideal client. A real photo. Snag it from their LinkedIn or other social media profile.
3. Caption the photo with their name.
4. Make a list of what you know about them. How old are they? What do they do for a living? Are they a student, parent, early in their career, or in later stages? How long have they worked? List as much as you can about their history.
5. What is your ideal client's problem—in their words? It's important that you consider the specific vocabulary and phrases they would use to describe their issue. You should be able to imagine those words coming out of their mouth. And be real. A single parent might say, "I need to make more money so I can send my kid to college." I doubt that they'd say, "I want to find resonance in my career."
6. Similarly what words and phrases would they use to describe their dream situation come true? Our single

parent from above might say, "I dream of watching my kid in a cap and gown getting her diploma," or "I dream about touring college campuses with my kid," or "I dream about not having to worry about buying schoolbooks my kid needs."

7. List the phrases (internet search strings) your ideal client might type into Google or another search engine to try to solve their problem. That single parent might type, "Remote jobs near me" or "How to ask your boss for more money" or "How to get a good-paying job."

It's important to get as clear as you can about what your ideal client does, earns, thinks, feels, and wishes for. Without this specificity, your marketing efforts will amount to shouting into the void. People will hear the noise, but nothing will land for them.

Creating a client avatar of your ideal client, on the other hand, means you can write marketing copy they can connect to. They'll feel heard. They'll feel seen. And they'll want to be coached by you.

As I mentioned when discussing niche, you'll likely end up coaching people who are not your ideal client. You'll think something is wrong with your marketing. "Why am I coaching a lot of married moms," says one of my clients, "when I help single moms?"

This is going to happen and when it does, *do not* change your niche.

One of the career coaches I trained told me she wanted to work with individuals with disabilities. Within her first month, she landed five new clients. She was elated—until she realized that none of them actually had disabilities, though they had family members or friends who did.

Convinced that her narrow niche "didn't work," she broadened her focus to: "I help people who would like a new job." Unsurprisingly, since this was basically everybody on the planet, nobody knew whether she was for them or not. Her leads went to zero. Nothing about her was unique. Nothing communicated her expertise.

She ended up going three months without any sales. As soon as she reverted back to being a career coach who helps individuals with disabilities get jobs, she landed clients again.

This raises an important distinction. Your ideal client avatar isn't always who you end up coaching. You end up coaching people who are attracted to how you market yourself.

Stick with your niche.

# CHAPTER SIX

# Making Magic

Career coaching isn't just about getting someone a job. It means helping them figure out their rightful place in the universe, their avocation. I like to frame it as what they're meant to do that lights them up and gives their life meaning.

Like I said in the last chapter, I'm pretty amazing at this. That sounds immodest, I know, but it's absolutely true. I have a kind of sixth sense when it comes to helping people figure out their calling.

When I was a recruiter, I'd be scanning through a thick stack of résumés when one would catch my eye. Why? Because I heard the words, "This is the one." It might be an unappealing, butt-ugly résumé overpacked with stale phrases and meaningless words, but for some reason my hand would stop mid-air as I was about to put it in the "maybe" stack.

It felt like an elemental force, like gravity. I'd be somehow pulled toward that résumé. When I'd call the applicant, they'd be miraculously able to pick up the phone in the only thirty-minute window of clear signal they'd get while driving to a tiny town near where they'd be hiking for the next two weeks in some remote somewhere or other.

"Wow, I'm so glad you called me right now," they'd say, amazed that I'd gotten through. And this person would end up being our next significant hire. They'd transform their division.

Today, when I help someone identify what they're meant to do, I experience this same weird kind of knowing. I might not get a single answer—I might hear myself suddenly spewing a bunch of random job ideas at them—but one of them will inevitably be The Job, the one that will light the fire in my client's heart and soul.

Among the hundreds of clients I've worked with, I have a 99.99 percent success rate in helping them identify and land a job in their chosen avocation. There's only one person who, at the end of our time together, didn't land on their chosen job. His name is Adam (because of course it is), and he remains the first I've not been able to help. My one and only.

You're probably asking, as have many others: What makes me so freakishly good at this? We've talked about this before: intuition.

There are mechanics and individual, itty-bitty steps that will help you and your client identify their path and their purpose, and I'll teach them to you. But I can guarantee you're going to flail around if you don't lean into your intuition. You want to access that inner part of you that's connected to the energy of something larger than yourself.

Some people call this the Universe. Others call it God. Whatever you call it, you must tap in if you want to be good at this. My process of tapping in might be a little more woo-woo than yours, and a deep dive into that is beyond the scope of this business book. What's most important is that you do it in a way that works for you.

Don't worry, this isn't all right-brain stuff. Once you've tapped in, you'll follow a step-by-step process I'll detail for you in the following pages.

## FINDING THEIR CAREER DIRECTION

Some clients already know exactly what they want to do. They have a specific new role in mind, or they want to step up to the next level of what they're doing now. Others may be a little more unsure of what their next steps may be. This next part is for the latter.

I know there's big magic afoot when a client is considering a career change. Those clients are being nudged in a different direction, though they may not know what it is yet. It's a humbling opportunity to help them find their areas of resonance, the role in alignment with who they are and what they want next. When I talk to these clients, I know I'm going to help them find a direction. And that moment when I see the light spark in their eyes—that's something beyond job satisfaction for me. It's proof that I have found my own purpose and calling in helping others find theirs.

Many clients have an inkling or daydream of where they'd like to go, and they just need some outside confirmation that they're not being unrealistic. My client Orlando is a great example. His family owns a company that refurbishes and rebuilds equipment so it can be resold. Orlando's father is the founder and CEO of the company, and Orlando himself is the owner's son—a VP and the heir apparent to the organization. Recently he got his master's degree in organizational design, a subject that fascinates him but that dovetails better with change management than it does the family business. Orlando has an idea—an inkling—of what he wants to do next.

Tom does too. Tom spent his entire career in hospital support services across the United States. Support services are non-core parts of care delivery ranging from environmental and food services to patient transport and services that back up the physicians and nurses delivering care. Tom isn't sure what he wants to do, but he's ready for a change. "Tom," I tell him, "I know we're going to land somewhere."

"How do you know?" he asks me.

"I have a 99.99 percent hit rate," I tell him.

Tom loves my track record, my confidence, and my assurances. He's relieved because he knows we're going somewhere—and he's been struggling with that for so long.

After we talk and work together a bit, Tom identifies that his goal is to become CEO of a small, rural hospital. Once we land on that together, he's over the moon. "There's no stopping me now," he tells me. "I know exactly what I'm going to do. I know exactly where I'm going to go."

Kim was a supervisor at an insurance company for farmers, but she left the company two years ago and has been taking courses. "Maybe I'll be a law secretary or administrative assistant," she tells me, confessing that she's always loved the idea of being a source of help and support.

Orlando, Tom, and Kim are good representatives of the clients you'll work with. Like them, your clients will come to you with varying degrees of certainty about their next steps.

It's not just my success rate that makes me know I'm going to land them where they want to be. It's because each of them—each of all of us—are what Co-Active Training Institute calls "naturally creative, resourceful, and whole." The answer to what's next for them isn't out there, in the work they've already done and the education they've obtained. The answer is within *them*. My job—and yours—is to help them think about things with a different part of their minds, by asking questions and taking them through activities that help them uncover what their what's-next might be.

## THE FOUR-STEP CAREER DIRECTION PROCESS

I want to teach you the process I use for helping people find their new career direction. I always start by telling my clients these caveats:

1. **Don't expect there to be one perfect answer.** I joke about people asking me what they should be when they grow up, but I actually dislike this question—especially when it's directed at kids. It sets the false expectation that there's just one answer when most of us have multiple careers in our lifetime. That's normal and perfectly okay. There's no tragedy in not working in the field dictated by your college degree. In fact, several studies indicate that less than thirty percent of people do. When I give

my clients permission to come up with more than one answer, they think more creatively. They dream bigger.

2. **This is not a passive activity.** We've all taken assessment and skills-based tests where you answer some questions and then boom, you learn you're supposed to be a veterinarian. This is not like that. It's an active endeavor. It requires energetic and mental movement, being willing to go someplace you've never gone before, if only in your mind.

3. **We're not looking for a single dot on a line.** Instead we're looking to identify the overlap in a Venn diagram made up of three circles. The first circle contains what your client is good at. The second is made up of what your client loves to do. And the third holds whatever's out there that will pay your client what they deserve. There's likely to be more than one thing in the intersection between all three. Help your client explore.

Here are the four phases I take clients through. Each client moves at their own pace. Sometimes I'll stay in one of the phases for a bit until they're ready to move on.

## STEP ONE: SITTING ON THE ROCK

I want my clients to spend some time sitting and thinking about what they want—not flapping away and taking ineffective action in directions that may or may not be the right ones. So I give them a mental image to make taking a pause easier: I ask that they imagine themselves sitting and pondering on a big rock.

While they're sitting on this metaphorical thinking rock, I ask them to consider 1) what they love to do and 2) what they're good at. These may not be the same things. You'll recognize them as two of the three circles in our Venn diagram of career direction.

There are three powerful but also fun activities I find very effective for job seekers looking at themselves through the *love to do/good at* lenses. I call them Chunks of Ten, List of Values, and Powerful Questions. I assign these as homework, and I recommend you work through them yourself right now, or come back to them when you're done with this chapter. Each of them will take about twenty minutes, and require nothing more than paper, a pen, and an open mind.

## Chunks of Ten

Write out at least ten memories of times when you felt powerful, alive, and successful over the course of your life—from the youngest you that you can remember up to right now. Once you're done—and not before then, even if it takes a few days to find those memories—look over what you've written, and see if you can find any themes or patterns. It may help to use colored markers or to draw lines between the things that connect to each other.

## List of Values

Looking at a list of personal core values can get you thinking about which are in alignment with who you are. There are a number of online resources to find a list like this and at the end of the book is my contact information. Reach out asking for my List of Values worksheet designed specifically for career. Wherever you find your list, print it out, and with two differently colored highlighters, mark in one color all the values that speak to you, that feel like "Oh, this is a must. This is so important to me." Using the other highlighter to mark all the ones that are definitely Not You.

## Powerful Questions

I came up with pointed questions about career direction for a book to which I contributed a chapter. The list includes things like: *Looking back at your career, when did you feel the most alive? What were you doing? Who was around you? What was your impact on them?* And: *If you had a billboard that 10,000 people passed every day, what would it say? What would it show?*

I'm sure you have different Powerful Questions as well. Work through them yourself at least once before handing them over to a client. Then ask them to sit on the rock and think them through.

## Put It All Together

Once you've completed these three exercises separately, take a look at all of them as a group and see if you can find any common themes. Sort those items into two of the Venn diagram's circles: "What I love to do" and "What I'm good at doing."

London Business School professor Herminia Ibarra wrote a book I highly recommend called *Working Identity*. In it she follows thirty or so people through their career transitions. I hoped I'd find a silver bullet in her text. What assessment did these people take that told them what they were supposed to do in their life?

Of course what Ibarra and I have separately concluded is that there really is no silver bullet, no magic assessment to help your clients identify this. I wish there were! It would make everyone's life so much easier. Every time I've taken a career assessment, the results tell me I should either be a bartender—clearly, no one has seen me try and fail to make a good martini—or a human resources executive. There's some value here; the assessments are picking up on the fact that I love to listen to people and help them find their way. But the questions are simply too rote and generalized to reveal that the actual role and tasks of a human resources executive, which I was for twenty years, made me really unhappy.

Steer your clients away from putting weight on quizzes and assessments. They aren't nuanced or wide-ranging enough to be helpful. In my experience the exercises and questions I've outlined in this chapter work really well—sometimes in a relatively short period of time. I've had conversations with clients in which they've identified a new career direction in ninety minutes. Others take something closer to a couple of weeks. The longest time it's taken any of my clients to find their way is a month.

Another book I highly recommend is *Escaping Career Prison* by Amy Van Court. She has some wonderfully effective exercises in there. One is similar to the Chunks of Ten. She also has a nice List of Values.

## STEP TWO: INTERACTIVE Q & A

In Step One, you and your client learned the general things they like to do and feel they're good at doing. But you'll need this next step to figure out how to translate that data into specific jobs and roles.

This is where knowing about many different roles is incredibly helpful to you. Perhaps you were an executive and have seen different roles in an organization. Or you were in human resources or a recruiter and hired different roles within organizations. Maybe you were a consultant and have worked with different types of roles within organizations. If you have none of this background, do your homework—read about common roles with organizations. Any and all of this helps you in being able to ask, "What about this job? And what about that job? Have you thought about this?"

First ask your client to walk you through their homework and tell you about what they love and are good at. Take good notes.

From there I go back to the very beginning of their career, starting from their first job all the way to today. I'm looking for the jobs they stayed with for a good chunk of time. Then I zero in. I ask them to envision themselves there at that company. I ask them to tell me a wee bit about their job there. And then I ask them to tell me two things:

1. The top three things they loved about that job, and
2. The top three things they hated about that job.

I'm looking for information about their tasks, their roles, and their responsibilities, not people or culture or mission. I want my client to focus on the actual work on their desk. "I loved that I was so valued for my help" doesn't tell me or them much that we can associate with another job. But "I loved leading facilitation sessions" does.

Kim, who was a supervisor at an insurance organization, tells me she loved customer service. It still isn't specific enough. Never accept something like that, a surface response. Dig deeper until you get to a task. I ask, "Tell me what you mean by customer service."

"I love being in the center," she says. "Where employees, other departments, they come to me for help. I love solving their problems and being reliable in their eyes to find answers to questions."

That isn't quite customer service if you think about it. But if you went with Kim's original answer, customer service, you'd miss a wide range of other jobs that Kim could enjoy doing.

Hearing Kim's other two loves elicits more. She loves law and anything dealing with regulations, codes, and rules. She also loves processes and procedures. She likes to follow them if they are written down somewhere and write them if they're not.

Then I ask, "What are the three things you really didn't like in that job?" Again, not people, not culture, not mission, but the actual work on her desk. I also don't mean things she could tolerate and do if she must. I am looking for the things that really pulled down her energy. Things she avoided or wanted to delegate whenever she could.

Here Kim says that she really hated blue-sky ideating, which is a loose, no-limits kind of brainstorming. It isn't what she loves. She'd rather be told what to do, and she'll do it. She also doesn't like very repetitive things, like the closing month's procedures a bookkeeper must do. And she really dislikes disharmony. She has a really hard time when people don't get along.

I continue, going from job to job. Listening to the role and writing down three loves and three hates. All the while jobs are popping in my head. Office manager. Paralegal. Accounting. Payroll manager. I don't share any of the jobs yet. Sometimes I end up crossing one out like payroll manager because the repetitive nature of processing payroll might be too repetitive for Kim.

Now that I have a full document of loves and hates and a small list of jobs, I jump to daydreams. I ask, "Do you ever dream about doing a job?" Or: "If you've won the lottery or were retired, what would you do?" And see if any of those things cause jobs to pop into my head.

At the end of our session, I share the list of jobs that come up for me with my client and give homework.

## STEP THREE: SOLO RESEARCH AND REFLECTION

After I share the list of five to ten jobs that come up for me during our conversation, I ask the client to look up three of them, and follow the same pattern and path that we just took with loves and hates. I ask them to list the top three things that sound amazing about that job and the top three things that sound terrible. It's also beneficial if they know someone who's been in that role and can chat with that person before we meet again. Sometimes clients are motivated to look at YouTube videos of people talking about the role, or do other kinds of online research.

One of the things I *don't* want them to do, however, is look at the job requirements. Even though they may not have the education or certification to do the job, I want them to ignore that for now. We're not at that point. We aren't trying to figure out how to get that job—we're trying to figure out if they want that job.

## STAGE FOUR: TOGETHER LANDING

We may go through another round of stages two and three before the client lands on their career direction.

When the client is all done with their research, I ask them to rank their loves and hates about each potential job while I take detailed notes. Sometimes there are two or three jobs they're really interested in. Sometimes there's only one. And sometimes I think of additional possibilities based on what they've said. If that happens, we go through another round of research and reflection.

But for ease of reference, let's say your client has chosen their top three ideal jobs. Now it's time to look at each position's requirements. What level of education is the employer seeking? Certifications? Experience?

The answers may change your client's rank. There's little point in continuing to research and plan for a job that requires many more years of experience or training than your client actually has.

It may be that your client is one or two jobs away from the ability to get that position. Kim, my client who worked decades in insurance, she lands on human resources manager. She has all of the credentials for the role but lacks full-desk recruiting skill—sourcing candidates all the way to negotiating offers. We agree that her next job should be as a human resources generalist with recruiting responsibilities. From there, she could be promoted to her Ideal Job of human resources manager.

When your client has their number one Ideal Job, they've landed. I know when this is so when I hear the client saying things like "I keep thinking about this one job." Or "I think I know what it is." Or "This one job, I'm really drawn to it."

Ask them if they can look back, knowing now what their Ideal job is, and ask when they look, can they see if perhaps it was all meant to be. That there was a path they took that brought them to where they are now.

The clients we've talked about would look like this:

Kim: from manager of an insurance company to HR manager.

Tom: from VP of Ancillary Services of many hospitals to CEO of a regional hospital system.

Orlando, VP of Operations and heir apparent to change management consultant.

Those are all clean trajectories that make sense. So much sense that they almost seem predestined, right?

That's magic.

# WHY IS KNOWING YOUR CLIENT'S IDEAL JOB SO IMPORTANT?

Of course it's a lot easier to get where you want to go if you know where that is. But another reason why it's vital that you know your client's Ideal job is that it's the secret to writing killer résumés and putting together highly effective dossiers.

Long ago I used to be a "regular" résumé writer. I was prolific—I worked on people's résumés day in and day out—but I was missing an important aspect of my client's career search. What if they don't want to keep doing what they've already done? Ninety-nine percent of my clients come to me wanting something slightly or even very different. And if I don't know that and take it into account, I'll miss a significant opportunity to position those clients differently.

Let's say a product manager is ready to become a director of product. (Yes, those are different jobs.) If I write a résumé thinking that all I have to do is highlight what they've already done, I'm only telling part of the story. I'm overlooking the opportunity to position them for their target job.

Another example: Kim, the insurance company supervisor who wants to become an HR manager. If all I talk about on her résumé is her skill in managing insurance claims, I miss the fact that she's hired thirty people and has trained almost two hundred others. Was hiring the main part of her job? No. But if I don't know what she's targeting, I might not even mention it.

Or Geoffrey. Geoff sends me his current résumé, which details a lot of amazing work in quality assurance and quality management. He was a supervisor at an organization called

StemCyte that does stem cell research. Before that, he was a quality assurance supervisor at a nutraceutical organization. Before that, he was an HR benefits assistant at United Water, and before that a retail specialist at an Apple Genius Bar.

During the career direction phase, one of the jobs I mention to Geoff is instructional designer—they're the ones who put together engaging education training programs, mostly in sales enablement but also in training departments. He's enthusiastic and wants to go for it.

Remember he was in quality assurance and quality management. The ideal job that he sent to me was for an instructional designer and trainer. If I didn't know what his ideal job was, I would've revised his résumé to make it an amazing one for a quality assurance/quality management role.

Even when the career pivot isn't that dramatic, it's still important that you understand it and reflect it in the client's résumé.

Sejal was in a dissatisfying job in finance. One day she was bored as usual and also annoyed that her paycheck was wrong again, so she got into the elevator to head upstairs and talk with the payroll manager. She was so obviously annoyed on the ride up that the person standing next to her in the elevator asked if she was okay. Sejal went off on the payroll department and how they didn't seem to be able to do something as simple as fix her benefits issue. Little did she know she was talking to the chief human resources officer (CHRO).

So when a job opened up, the CHRO offered a job to Sejal. And off she went. She has joined four startups since, rising very quickly from HR manager to HR director. Each startup had a very happy financial outcome. Her current startup went IPO, and she was involved in many of the major tasks as the VP of HR. What does she want to do now? She wants to be a consultant to a venture capitalist firm. If I didn't know that, I'd write an amazing résumé for a stellar chief human resources officer for a startup—not a consultant.

Last story, and this one is an even smaller pivot: Andrew. Andrew is a director of product. He's been a director of product for many years in the world of educational technology. He wants a VP role or maybe even a chief product officer in edutech. If I create an amazing director-level résumé it might serve him well, but I bet it will look too low-level. Not strategic enough. Now that I know he wants to be CPO, I can ask him questions about times when he led strategy and worked on top-level projects to highlight his strategic and end-to-end capabilities in delivering product through a team.

Now you know the secret, and it's a magic carpet ride for your clients. Knowing first where they're going and seeing an actual, real job posting, you can now create something that's truly rich and aligned so that whoever reads it gets them and understands at a glance that they're perfectly suited for the role.

Don't be a regular résumé writer. There are already far too many of those. Get insanely good at writing résumés. I did, and next to helping people land on their forever jobs, it's one of my biggest assets as a career coach.

As you read about steps and processes, don't forget to play your hunches and listen to your gut. You know more than you think you do, especially if you pay attention with all your senses. And that includes the sixth sense.

# CHAPTER SEVEN

# The Dossier—Weaving Magic from Data

Lordy, people hate writing their résumés. And as an ex-recruiter I can see when you hate it because I'm forced to read it, and I'm hating reading it with you. I deeply wish you'd delegated this responsibility to someone else.

We need to get away from the myth that you must write your own résumé. It flies in the face of everything we know in business. What seat do you occupy on the proverbial bus? Is this your core competency? Asked another way: Has anyone ever told you, "Oh my goodness, you're an amazing writer"? Do you find it easy to write about yourself?

If not, delegate it.

What about design? Are you amazeballs at it? Like desktop jury-rigging Microsoft Word to look like something out of Canva design?

If my clients are a negatory on any of the above, then I highly recommend they delegate this arduous painful task to someone else. Someone like me. And perhaps you.

## I GEEK OUT OVER RÉSUMÉS

Thank the heavens we're all made differently. Me, I love a good résumé.

A good résumé tells the story that hiring managers, like I used to be, want to hear. Stepping back into those shoes, I want to know the arc of your life journey that brought you to this singular point, the point at which I'm meeting with you and saying: *we want to hire you.*

I don't want to keep on reading résumés and interviewing prospects. I want to find someone to fill this job, and do it fast so I can get back to other things. So I'm reading your résumé with great hope: will you be the one who lets me off this hiring hook?

Your résumé (called a curriculum vitae in some countries) is key. It's basically the Brochure of You. And it requires serious command of writing, editing, and design.

I'm going to teach you the basics of how you can help your clients delegate this painful task to you, their career coach. This translates into higher coaching fees because this is the number one task job seekers want to have done for them and will pay cold, hard cash to do so. But it also means you'll need to be better than the sea of average résumé writers. And that sea is vast.

I'm going to teach you what makes an exceptional résumé as well as how it's the foundation of a stellar dossier: résumé, cover letter, and LinkedIn profile. I'm keeping this basic because if I went deep on this subject, you'd bounce out of here fast. So I'm going to tell you just enough for you to be a notch above the rest of the résumé writers out there—but not so much that you'll be drowning in boredom and tears.

Writing an extraordinary résumé requires that you tap once again into your particular brand of magic—your intuition—in order to weave the threads that make up your client's job journey into a cogent and magnetic career path. The one that leads them directly to their future employer's door. The one that results in that future employer exclaiming, "Oh my goodness, we've found the right hire!"

## Two Top Mistakes People Make

Back when I was in charge of hiring, I made offers to professionals who presented with what I thought were horrible résumés, but it didn't happen often. A candidate with a weak résumé would've had to really blow us away during the interview process—assuming that their subpar résumé was enough to get them an interview at all. There's no doubt about it: a bad résumé makes the job search an uphill climb.

You'd think by the time someone is at the C-suite level they'd have an amazing résumé, but that is so not the case. Long ago, when I worked at AMN Healthcare, we were doing a C-suite level search for the chief human resources officer, and the top candidate had a résumé better suited for a mid-level professional. She came highly recommended by someone the CEO respected in the field, and she sounded amazing over the phone, but she still didn't get the job. Our CEO continued to ask me to present other candidates all the way up until we were performing background checks, all because her résumé was weak.

This candidate made several of the following mistakes, all of which I've seen and grieved when I was in recruiting. These are the main culprits that get hiring managers wondering if the job seeker is the right one all the way through the interview process.

**It looks all wrong.**

I rarely let clients pick the format for their résumé. They're too close to the process, and they get overly attached to a look and feel that may not be appropriate. One example: a woman going for a VP of Product position sends me a sample of a format she's in love with. It's pink with cute, curly lettering. There is no way I'm going to let her go with this. Instead I pick a format that works for her at her professional level and for her location. Note: the format that works in New York City is not the same as the one that works in Nashville, Tennessee.

Length is also part of the at-a-glance consideration a hiring manager will give a résumé. There are general rules here: a one-pager for a new grad, two pages for a professional, and many pages for a seasoned job seeker presenting a curriculum vitae. Bobble the appropriate length for the level of experience and the position, and the job seeker may get booted out of the race from the get-go. There are additional nuances here too. If an executive recruiting firm is involved, a submitted résumé might be a one-pager or a four-pager based solely on their whims.

**It reads like an HR document.**

Let's be honest here: résumés are often boring. But they needn't be—and they shouldn't be. A great résumé pulls the reader forward, taking them through the arc of a compelling story to an inevitable conclusion: this candidate is The One. The one who will help the hiring manager and their company reach their goals, achieve their dreams, and live happily ever after.

It's impossible for it to do that if it reads like a dull policy and procedure document. Or the world's most boring autobiography. Or if it's dense and packed with so many bullet points the reader loses interest.

A great résumé is a marketing piece, and it needs to be written that way. Just like a good brochure, landing page, or ad, it should excite and interest the reader enough that they want to learn more.

And what do marketing experts do before creating a campaign? They identify their ideal client: their target.

## YOUR CLIENT'S TARGET

The most important piece of information you need from your client, the one that makes writing their résumé significantly easier, is a target: the job they're going after and, by extension, the person who's going to receive and review the document. And it's why most job seekers get stuck writing their own résumés. They have no idea how to identify who the target is and what that target wants.

In advertising, you have to know who you're targeting—how they think, what they want, what they fear most, and the language they use to describe it—in order for your message to land. Without identifying the target, the one person you're crafting that ad campaign for, you have no idea what to write or how to write it. But once you clearly and cogently identify your target reader, you'll know exactly what to say.

The ideal reader starts with identifying the ideal job. This should be an actual job posting, one your client finds for you that was posted by a real company for whom your client would like to work. The listing should be relatively complete, meaning that the job posting includes requirements for the position, educational background sought, years of experience needed, etc.

Your client may struggle to find even one. Or they may send you two or three. If they do, ask your client which one floats to the top for them. They can always apply to the other roles later, but it's best to focus on just one of them for now. That's because when you focus on just one job, you can write a high-quality résumé relatively quickly.

Make sure you give your client a specific and quick deadline to get this job posting back to you because some clients take a long time to research this and feel good about it. Those clients will want to make it perfect. It doesn't need to be perfect. Give them just one or two days to complete this assignment.

Once you have your client's ideal job and anything you can find about who's doing the hiring, it's time to collect the other items you need in order to start writing. These include your client's current résumé, the résumé template you want to use, a list of action verbs, and a completed list of questions, which we'll discuss below.

## LIST OF QUESTIONS (LOQ)

Don't assume that what's on your client's old résumé is accurate. Instead, use a list of questions (I call mine the LOQ) to help you tell a story that fills the gap between where they are now and where they want to be. Giving your client your LOQ to fill out means all the relevant information you need will be in a single document, organized specifically to speed up the writing process.

My list, which is a template I've modified over the years, is made up of all the questions that come to my mind as I contrast and compare the client's old job and their new ideal job. It essentially asks the client to detail their experience, skills, and abilities in each of their previous roles as seen through the lens of their ideal job. Hit me up if you'd like a copy of the LOQ.

If the ideal job is one of customer success, for example, then my LOQ directs them to give me information about their past jobs as it relates to customer success. Where and how were they already developing the skills they'll need in this new job? Once you have that information, you can write their résumé based on what the target company—and the target reader—is looking for.

Yes, this does mean that if your client has tons of supply chain experience, but the target company doesn't care anything about that, you won't lead with that experience on their résumé. This is surprising to a lot of jobseekers, who often believe that the more stuff they cram into their résumés, the better.

A killer résumé doesn't bore its reader (the recruiter or hiring manager) with data they don't care about. Instead it answers their questions before they even ask them. By including only what's necessary you save them valuable time, and you showcase what's most important: the relevant and closely aligned experiences the job requires.

Andrew was laid off nine months ago. By the time he calls me, he feels like something's wrong with him. Actually what's amiss is his dossier. He was a VP and top P&L leader of a consulting firm, but his résumé makes him look like an entry-level operator. It's in the wrong format, it's the wrong length, and it's written as a "been there, done that" document. It shows little or no impact Andrew made in his previous positions.

Once he sees his new résumé, he says, "Is this me?" He's so excited he sends his new résumé to all of the people he already talked to in the past few months. Almost immediately he gets a call back congratulating him on his résumé and scheduling a screening call.

Andrew is now the executive director of his city's development division, and I get regular pictures of his family on vacation—something they hadn't been able to afford for over a year.

## GETTING YOURSELF READY TO WRITE

First: breathe. Writing someone else's résumé is significantly easier than writing your own. Recognizing that will help you get over any residual résumé-writing trauma you may have from your own job-seeking journey.

Next: practice. It takes about a year of résumé-writing before you'll begin to feel like you're getting the hang of it. Lean into curiosity and mastery, and know that you're going to be bad at it for a while before you slowly get good at it. Like all writing, résumé-writing is a craft. Don't be discouraged by all the editing and tweaking you'll find yourself doing. It's part of the process.

Last: tap in. You also need to love your clients. There I said it—love—in a business book. There are résumé-generating shops where writers never get to meet or know the jobseekers, and that makes it hard for them to channel those jobseekers and their voices. You, however, will be able to get to know your clients. You'll learn their dreams and their challenges. You'll fall in love with them, and in the process imbue each word of their résumés with aspirations, hopes, and beliefs in their abilities. By the time you're done writing, that résumé is a love letter from you to your client—and from them to the company they hope will hire them.

Jessica Aebi, one of our career coach graduates, tells me that she wasn't excited about "having" to write résumés, but she loves it now. When she sits down to write, she thinks about her client and all that they want in their career and life, and it gives her a good deal of joy to write about it. This, too, is magic.

# CHAPTER EIGHT

# The Magic of the Right Strategy

*If you fail to plan, you're planning to fail.*
~ Benjamin Franklin

"What does 'ideal' look like to you?" I ask my client. Christine is—or was—CXO for an eGaming company. She's what I call a unicorn; it's unusual to find a woman in a top spot in eSports. Christine is sitting in a gaming chair sporting the logo of League of Legends, one of the teams under her company's umbrella. She's muscular and thin, with short, platinum-blonde hair and a sharp, infectious wit.

"That's the thing," she says in her raspy voice. "I know more of what I don't want than what I do want."

Christine's company was bought by a large global company

that installed a new boss in charge of her division. Within a month, he'd brought in two of his favorite sidekicks. One day, without any warning, he shows her the door.

"For the first time in my twenty-plus-year career, I've been kicked out on my [beeping-beep]," Christine says drily. "I am hugely embarrassed and utterly pissed."

What Christine doesn't realize is that at the C-suite level, getting fired is kind of a thing. This revolving door of "opportunities" is a side effect of constant ownership turnover. A new owner comes in, and a department is let go. A new boss brings in their buddies from another company. A new CEO steps into his new office, and the first thing he does is fire half the SVPs. It's the way of corporate America, and the fact that Christine hasn't experienced it yet is astonishing. To me, she's a rock star.

From her perspective, however, she's stuck. She can't think about getting another job when all she can think about is how angry she is at her former boss. She can't imagine working elsewhere when she's focused on how she was treated. It's been nine months since she was unceremoniously fired. What Christine needs is a strategy.

People like Christine—successful, goal-oriented, and motivated—react to having a strategy by immediately falling into their lane. Give them a checklist, and their mojo kicks in. I share my strategy with Christine, and the needles in her eyes are replaced by curiosity.

"Maybe the best way to stick it to them is to get an amazing job!" she exclaims. Sweet. Now we're talking.

Christine is far from alone in feeling lost without a

job-seeking strategy. Along with putting together a résumé and preparing for interviews, strategy is one of the top three places clients get stuck. We've talked about the former and will discuss the latter, but for now, let's focus on how to create a plan for getting their name out there. And, even more importantly, how to keep your clients motivated and on track.

Wait, don't they want a new job? If they've gotten fired, like Christine, don't they *need* one? Yes, yes, they do. But no matter how much clients may want a new job—to be happier, to earn more money—they get overwhelmed by the many tasks seeking a new job requires.

This is where you come in, with the perfect strategy to get them over their hurdles. You're their best chance of getting unstuck and motivated. Especially if you charge them a decent amount. A significant investment in the process encourages them to actually do the work.

We humans have an uncanny knack for putting obstacles between us and the very things we want the most. Networking? Ugh, we have better things to do. In fact even the most mundane of tasks can suddenly seem more important than doing the work to find a new job.

And oh, the creativity of the justifications and excuses!

I'm taking a vacation.
I just got a three-month contract gig.
I'm busy rearranging all of the furniture in my home.
I decided to repaint my bathroom.
I just adopted a puppy, and I'm too tired from house-training.
I am going back to school.

I need to take a certification course.

I need to take care of my mom.

I need to move my child into their college dorm.

I'm pregnant and I have baby brain.

I'm thinking of buying a franchise.

I'm getting married.

I'm getting divorced.

I've seen this so, so often that I've realized that this is something that simply happens once someone decides to get a new job. Everything else suddenly vies for their attention—and wins. Because of this, I've developed a grab bag of magic tricks to help you get your clients unstuck and execute a focused job search.

## TELL THEM WHAT TO EXPECT

In my introduction video, I warn my new clients of the way all the things will suddenly crop up in their lives and beg them not to do the work of a job search. I say, "I have a word of warning for you. There's something that almost always happens once I start working with a client, and that is that you will go from a very boring life to all of a sudden having a million things you need to do. You'll want to take a vacation, take care of a sick parent, get married, get divorced, get pregnant, have a baby, worry that you're having a baby, get a new puppy, insert the issue. Why does this happen? Because it's as if the universe sees that you're finally doing something for yourself for once, and will begin to try to distract you. Because focusing on yourself is hard. It's risky."

This warning is often enough to help my clients recognize that whatever's in front of them is the universe trying to draw their attention away from seeing what's actually happening.

## GO TO MARKET: THE THREE-LEGGED STOOL

Once your client has their dossier in their hands, it's time to execute a go-to-market strategy. This is where many people get stuck. When I ask people in my sales calls, "What's the strategy you've been using to find your ideal job?" I'm often met with silence or a string of busywork or the words, "I don't have one."

Then I share my strategy. My strategy is straight from the MBA marketing playbook, and I like to describe it to clients as a three-legged stool. By this I mean that if the client—and you—neglect to tackle the career marketplace in all three areas, your job search seat is incomplete and unstable. Translation: it has a reduced chance of actually working. It will take longer than necessary for your client to find the right job.

I led talent acquisition for several companies and carefully tracked where the best candidates came from. I combined that data into three major channels—the legs of the stool. These were where I found the best candidates, and they are also where your client must be represented. The first leg is the lowest hanging fruit, and it's also what most people do first: apply to online job postings. The second leg is to reach out to their own network. The third leg is making use of executive recruiters. Each leg requires a different approach. Together they make up your client's go-to-market strategy for their job search.

## Online Job Sites and Postings

There are three main kinds of job sites: aggregator sites, company job postings, and paid job sites.

Aggregators are sites that scrape the internet and compile all the job postings they find into a one-stop shopping place. Most people think of indeed.com, but searches there often elicit job titles that don't necessarily match skills or listings that all sound alike—and sometimes the jobs or links have expired. I prefer Google for Jobs, which uses machine learning to match your client's search with job descriptions, not just job title. It also tells you whether the position is still open.

Most companies have open job listings somewhere on their website, often under the heading careers or opportunities. Once your client applies for a job there, they will most likely be put into what's called an applicant tracking system (ATS) that uses pre-established screening questions to distinguish between unqualified applicants and viable candidates.

One or more of these questions will be what I call a knockout question. That's a question that, if answered incorrectly, will knock the candidate out of the running. Could be the extent of education or experience; could be something else. And it may not be obvious which question it is. In other words, your client will have no way of knowing if they're answering in a way that will get their résumé seen.

Paid job sites are where companies pay to have their job openings listed. There are paid sites for almost every job segment out there: nonprofits, government jobs, higher education, HR jobs. A good example of a paid job site is LinkedIn. The advantage of applying here is that it's a sure bet the job is still open. No company will knowingly continue to spend even a dollar on a listing if the job is no longer open.

All three of these job sites—aggregators, company sites, and paid sites—offer the ability to save your search and set up an alert to receive an email when there's a match. This is one way in which these sites can actually work well for your client.

A word of caution about job sites: if your client is in stealth mode, they may not want to upload their résumé anywhere except a company career site, where it's unlikely their current company's recruiter will stumble across them and realize they're looking to leave.

## Networking

Unless your client is in a field that requires leveraging relationships, like sales or politics, they're probably not skilled at networking. Most people think they need to join some meetup group or attend a social event or spend hours on LinkedIn trying to find a second- or third-degree connection and hope that someone will respond to them. These aren't effective ways to network.

Instead I ask clients to list at least twenty of their closest friends and family regardless of what field those people work in. Then I ask them to reach out to each person on their list just as they normally would. If they're a caller, call them. If they're a texter, text them. Reach out to them with one purpose and one purpose only: just to reconnect—about an upcoming holiday, the weather, whatever there is to talk about. Don't force the conversation. If the conversation moves to career, and many of them will, your client can let their contacts know that they're thinking about making a change and tell them what they're looking for.

About ten percent of the time, these conversations will result in a recommendation that your client chat or follow up with someone specific. That means that out of those twenty people, two reach-outs will result in more conversations. Of course the longer the initial list your client can make, the more potential there is.

There's another way your client can make good use of their network, and that's when they're applying for the low-hanging fruit: jobs posted online. When they come across one they're really excited about, I recommend they find someone to put in a good word for them—ideally someone who actually works at the company, but if not that, then someone listed in their network. Say Christine's BFF is the Chief Financial Officer for a really cool, widely known startup. Christine is eyeing a role at a global philanthropic company helping women in tech. I recommend that Christine's BFF send an email directly to the CFO equivalent at the target company. That email will land on the desk of a peer—and as if by magic, it will find its way to the recruiter. That recruiter will see the email chain as a referral. And when it comes to a job search, referrals are gold. They almost guarantee someone will look at your client's résumé, and maybe even give them a call. This, my friends, is how people get jobs. I have a secret for you: recruiters blast job opportunities on aggregators to get the word out because what they want most of all is a referral. Let that one sink in.

### Executive Recruiters

Executive recruiters can be independent agents or can work for a staffing firm like Korn Ferry, the world's largest executive search firm. They contract with a company to fill open positions and get paid either by finder's fee or retainer. A good solopreneur headhunter can make a million dollars a year—or more—because they solve a major pain point for companies who need top talent, which requires a lot of time-consuming research and vetting.

I tell my clients to keep their reach-outs to recruiters short, positive, and professional: "Hi, my name is Cara Heilmann. I got your name from a colleague. She said that you place marketing executives in this field. If so, please give me a call. My phone number is …" They should be sure to mention if this is a confidential, stealth search.

Careful. There are scams and fake executive recruiters out there. A genuine professional will not ask for money from your client, but a scam artist might ask to get paid for a "résumé review" or charge a "placement fee." Run away. Your client should never have to pay for the services of an executive recruiter.

## WHEN CLIENTS ARE RELUCTANT: OUTRAGEOUS OPTIONS

Jane is probably the most memorable client I've ever worked with. She was a brilliant director of product management for an Ivy League school who started drinking a glass of red wine at the start of each of our client calls. "It's four o'clock somewhere," she'd say. Within fifteen minutes, I could no longer understand her, and she couldn't remember what she was going to say, but that's not the only thing that made Jane memorable. The other thing was that she adopted one of my outrageous ideas.

Jane wanted a new job, but she hated everything about the job search process, and Jane wasn't inclined to do anything she didn't want to do. I wasn't going to recommend she deviate from my three-legged stool go-to-market plan, so I had to get creative. I needed to find a way to move Jane forward without her participation.

And then it hit me: many entrepreneurs hire virtual assistants to help them with admin minutia and other business tasks they despise. Why couldn't a jobseeker do the same? Jane insisted that every part of the job search process right up to the interview made her skin crawl. So I recommended she work with an agency and find a virtual assistant who could do the legwork for her.

Jane landed a great VA. And that VA scoured the internet looking for jobs that met Jane's criteria. She even went so far as to fill out job applications in draft form so Jane could come behind her, make edits, and press submit. The VA reached out to executive recruiters, and even researched people in Jane's network who she could send notes to and ask to recommend her. That VA got so good at it, all Jane needed to do was spend an hour a day on her job search and then show up for the interviews.

Needless to say, Jane got the job of her dreams. And I learned another way to make magic.

# CHAPTER NINE

# The Magic of Confidence

Confidence and personal charisma can make the difference between a pass and a job offer. But just because your client is introverted or shy doesn't mean they're doomed. I believe these are learnable skills, and I teach them to my clients every day.

Meet Manuel, who comes into my life by email with the subject line: "Help me."

"Dear Cara," he writes, "I need your help. I get two, maybe three calls from recruiters a week, but I can't get an offer. I think I'm cursed. Manuel."

It turns out that not only can't Manuel get an offer, he also can't even get past the initial call from the many recruiters who reach out to him. Curious, I open his LinkedIn profile. There he is, grinning so big it almost looks like he's laughing. Just looking at his face, I smile. And when I scan his profile, I see why recruiters are calling him. He knows an impressive number of software languages and he has a solid GitHub account.

I schedule a chat, and the moment I get him on the phone I can tell why he never advances in the interview process. We have a stilted, uncomfortable conversation punctuated by one-word answers and long, awkward pauses. "If I never have to talk with a person again, I'd be thrilled," says Manuel. "I know code, not conversation."

Manuel gives me an idea. I wonder if someone like him can improve their communication skills through acting, improv, and standup comedy techniques. It's because of Manuel that I start taking improv classes around the Bay area, and eventually Steve Martin's Standup Comedy Masterclass. Since then I've integrated ideas from Sylvia Hewlett's book on Executive Presence and Decker Communications' public speaking course to release the magic that is in each one of us. Let me share the ingredients of the tincture so you can help your clients grow their charisma and confidence.

## THE POWER OF STORYTELLING

I'm watching Gabriel Iglesias on Netflix. He's a very funny standup comedian who favors brightly colored Aloha shirts and whose identifying line is "I'm not fat, I'm fluffy." He describes his act like this: "I don't get controversial. I don't get political, and I don't tell you what to do with your life. I just tell stories, and you relate to them."

His stories are hysterical. I am on the edge of my seat and laughing for his entire set.

Everyone loves a good story. In fact storytelling is such a powerful communication tool that it's widely used in business in both external marketing and internal leadership. A story connects us to the speaker, making it more likely that we'll buy what that speaker is selling and follow them where they want us to go.

In a job search, connecting with a recruiter and the hiring team is an assured way to get a job offer. And because interviews are conversations, the more skilled your client is in the art of storytelling, the more engaging they'll be as a candidate. I've also heard from clients that storytelling has helped them in their roles after they land the job.

When we put our listener in the picture by helping them see what we're talking about in their mind's eye, they can absorb what we're saying much more easily than if we just said it. I could have simply told you that some comedian says his act isn't political or prescriptive, he just tells stories people can relate to. It's the same point I made above, but you wouldn't likely remember it. Instead I told you a story and painted a picture of fluffy Gabriel in his Aloha shirt and me, perched on the edge of my seat and laughing my patootie off. Now you have a scene in your mind to help anchor what I said. You're more likely to remember what I said—and me.

When someone gives us a visual we can picture, we find it easier to digest and hang onto the information they impart. So learn how to be a storyteller—and help your clients do the same. They'll make a powerful impression in their interviews, and they'll start getting offers.

This is my favorite part of coaching because the results are almost instantaneous. Turn a client into a storyteller, and they'll see that recruiters start responding right away. They'll see leaders who are very excited about bringing them on board. This is a powerful skill you're giving them, not just for the job search but for the rest of their lives.

I learned some of the techniques I'm about to teach you during my time as an executive coach for a large healthcare firm. But as I mentioned, I took it further on my own, adding several different improv courses and Steve Martin's master class. The biggest thing I learned from the latter is that while storytelling must appear effortless and off the cuff, it's important to be prepared. "If you want to sound spontaneous," Martin says, "you must write it all down, edit it, and practice and practice and practice."

Here are the three steps I recommend clients follow to become stronger storytellers during the interview process:

1. **Write out the answers to expected interview questions by hand.** Writing in longhand engages the brain differently than typing. We're more creative. We're also more likely to write how we talk instead of sounding formal and stuffy.

2. **Edit those answers down.** Cut out repetition and superfluous, unnecessary sections, whittling each answer down to sixty seconds or less when spoken aloud.

3. **Replace descriptions with vivid words or scenes.** "I lead meetings" is boring and unremarkable. "I'm the one in front of the room leading the meeting" paints a vivid

picture that puts the listener in the scene. They can now picture you leading, which is far more powerful than simply understanding that you've got that experience. "I'm a creative writer" is boring. "When I write, people tell me, 'Wow, Cara, you're such a creative writer'" is vivid. "I lead a team for a large company with multiple locations" is boring. But this is vivid: "I'm the staffing director at AMN Healthcare, a large national staffing agency with over 500 million in revenue. I lead a recruiting team of 25 recruiters in two states, Texas and California. We fill over 1,500 positions each year."

## EXUDING CHARISMA

Have you ever met someone who is charismatic, confident, engaging? A charismatic person is someone who displays both social and leadership skills. They exude warmth and competence that make them compelling and magnetic. Charisma confers stage presence—the kind that translates to the podium, the boardroom, and the job interview.

You don't have to be an extrovert to be charismatic. Both extroverts and introverts can learn and develop qualities that draw people to them. Here's how.

### Make the Other Person Look Brilliant

This is a fundamental principle of improv, but it might seem counterintuitive in a job interview. Shouldn't the candidate be the one who looks good?

Yes of course they should. But when we can master the ability to make the other person look good, we end up looking good too. In improv making the other person look good means continuing to throw assists while on stage. An assist doesn't mean spouting funny lines or cracking the audience up. It means setting up the other person to deliver the punchline.

In a job interview, throwing an assist means being other-focused. This is key to charisma, and highly misunderstood. True charisma isn't about being charming half as much as it's about making the other person—in this case, the interviewer—feel charming. The social warmth that comes from that is worth far more than any number of laughs earned.

Making others look good requires listening to what they're saying, not getting up in our heads worrying about what we're going to say next. It requires us to be emotionally attuned to the other person in the conversation. Saying things like, "Speaking to that point you just made," or "I'm curious to know your thoughts."

## Four Words

This is a game that comes from the world of improv and is meant to teach how to listen instead of rehearsing what you're going to say next. Participants stand in a circle, and one person starts with four words. The next person then must add to those four words—but with only four more words—and the sentence they create together must be complete and make sense. The next person adds four more words, and so on. The goal is to keep the sentence going as long as possible, and the only rule is that the sentence must continue to make sense.

It might go like this:

Person 1: I am excited that
Person 2: you are wearing purple
Person 3: gloves that shine in
Person 4: the dark so that
Person 1: your dog can follow
Person 2: your hands and dance
Person 3: to the midnight moon
Person 4: under the twinkling stars.

This game makes it impossible for you to think of what you're going to say until the very last word is said by the person before you. It teaches you to stop overthinking. If you try to anticipate, you choke. The goal is to listen and react in a moment, and it's a perfect game to teach clients who get stuck in their heads overthinking during job interviews and other conversations.

## Numbers

This is another improv game intended to help participants get out of their heads and connect to others in the room. Participants stand shoulder to shoulder in a circle facing outward. One at a time, each person will speak out a number in sequence beginning with number one and continuing with two, three, four, etc., but they must call out in random order—without creating a pattern or giving a hint like taking a big breath that they're about to speak.

The play continues until two or more people say the same number at the same time. When that happens, everyone claps and makes note of the number reached. The goal is to get to as high a number as possible without speaking at the same time.

I've played this in groups of varying sizes, and the highest I've seen the number go is 45. This game teaches people to listen to the movements of the room and to reach out with their senses to be attuned to everyone else playing. It's a great way to learn how to anticipate conversation and stop interrupting.

## Big and Small

Clinical research shows that our moods can be influenced by our movements. If we're sad and we're curled up in a ball on a bed, chances are we're going to continue to feel sad. Yet if we're sad and we stand up and march around or dance, our mood will tend to lift.

This has more direct application to a job search than simply cheering us up. When we're in a phone conversation with a potential employer, we want to come across with enthusiasm and confidence even though they can't see us. One way we can do that is to be big. And that's what this game is about.

In an improv class, it would work like this. You'd sit in a chair onstage facing the audience, and your improv partner would sit in another chair to your right—also facing the audience. Your job is to be physically big without making a sound or getting out of your chair. Your partner's job is to be small.

After fifteen or so seconds of this—and you can imagine how funny it looks—the instructor says to switch. You slowly transform from being big to being small, and your partner does the reverse.

You don't have to be in an improv class or have a partner to do this. Try it. And when you do, notice how you feel emotionally when you're being big as opposed to how you feel when you're being small. Research shows that when we feel big, we feel good and confident. When we feel small, we feel hidden, young, shy.

Think about how you want to sit in your chair in a job interview. Big or small?

## Voice Control

Studies show that when we speak slowly, we come across as more intelligent and believable than when we speak really fast. Similarly we think of people with higher voices as sweet and maybe soft, while we find people with lower voices commanding and dominant.

This game stretches vocal range so you can be mindful and in charge of how you're coming across. The first part of the game is to record yourself speaking at three different rates of speed. Open any book near you and record yourself reading a paragraph at your normal speed. Then read it again really fast, and one more time really slowly. Play your recording back and consider: at which speed do you sound the most charismatic and confident?

Next try the same thing, only varying your pitch. Record yourself reading the same paragraph at your normal pitch, then higher, then lower. How do you sound to yourself when you play it back? Who would you be more likely to hire?

By being aware of your vocal control, you can become better at communicating at varying speeds and pitches to support your message and your communication.

## Q-E-R

This is an enunciation exercise that's a little hard to describe in a book. But do it with me, and you'll see what I mean. Say the letter Q, clearly and almost explosively. Feel your diaphragm flex? You can also feel that Q in the back of your throat.

Now move into saying the letter E. You can feel it in the back of your throat, too, and you're making a face like you're flossing your own teeth.

Finally, say the letter R. This is like gargling in the back of your throat, almost like you're retching.

Q-E-R, Q-E-R. You want to do that five times in a row and only once a day, or you're going to damage your vocal cords. This exercise opens up your palate and exercises parts of your vocal cords that don't normally get a workout. This is really good for clients who mumble, slur, or swallow their words.

*   *   *

When you integrate improv principles and exercises into your career coaching practice, you can help your clients become more engaging during the interview process and improve their warmth and connection to others.

As for Manuel? Once I start working on all of the above with him, he immediately starts getting hiring manager interviews and lands a wonderful job at Netflix.

# EXECUTIVE PRESENCE

Back when I was slogging away in corporate America, one of my responsibilities was to coach high-potential leaders. Each year our company would identify 67 of them. We called them "HI-POs," and these high potentials were told they were going to attend "Cara's charm school."

We knew these leaders had the skills, the abilities, and the track records to be top leaders with our company, but something in the way they communicated was getting in the way of others seeing it. It was my job to work with them to develop executive presence.

Executive presence is made up of what you say, how you say it, and what you look like while doing so. And possessing it is more rare than you might think.

## What You Say

The key here is preparation, much like we do with our clients in nailing interviews by writing down, editing, and integrating storytelling. But how can you prepare for an event on the fly, like a quick meeting?

One of my classmates from grad school, Adena Friedman, is the CEO of NASDAQ. Email didn't exist back when she started out. Instead businesspeople wrote memos in Word, printed them out, stuck them in a yellow interoffice envelope, and sent them through the interoffice mail. Adena told me she liked that process a lot. She said it helped her clarify her thoughts so that when she entered a meeting, she knew just what she wanted to convey.

We can do the same today. Before your next meeting, take five or ten minutes and write down the answers to two questions:

1. What do you want the person or people you're meeting with to know?
2. What do you want them to feel?

And that's it. Once you write that out, you're prepared to share what's on your mind in a way that controls the outcome of that meeting.

## How You Say It

Do you murmur or mumble? Consider the Q-E-R exercise we talked about a moment ago. Do you have crutch words like um or uh? Eliminate them by adding awareness and a negative reinforcement like having a friend reach over and lightly snap a rubber band on your wrist every time you use a crutch word. Do you look up when you're thinking? Train yourself to look down. Do you have a really breathy or nasal voice? Do you speak too fast? Too slow? Record yourself speaking and consciously work to breathe, lower your register, and pace your speech.

## How You Look

This isn't about physical beauty. This is about projecting confidence and an air of leadership. And there are so many things that can undermine it: touching your hair, face, or neck. Tilting your head. Looking up, or darting your eyes around the room.

The best thing you can do for yourself and your clients is help them practice. Encourage them to train their bodies so they have a muscle memory of what it feels like to sit still and yet relaxed, balanced, and comfortable.

Don't forget basic self-care and hygiene. Does your client have a groomed hairstyle and look interview-ready? Is their wardrobe appropriate and well-maintained? An interview can fall apart over something as small as scuffed and dirty shoes.

Many of your clients' interviews will take place over Zoom or another video call service. Not only must they be camera-ready, but their setup needs to be ready too. Make sure they have:

- a strong Wi-Fi connection—if possible, have them connect directly to their router or modem.
- good sound quality—do they need a microphone? Is their wireless ear pod cutting in and out? Do they sound tinny or too far away?
- a professional video setup—is their head touching the top of the screen so they don't look small? Are they at eye level so they're not looking up or down into the camera? Make sure your client has a ring light to diffuse the lighting, and that they look directly into the camera, not the interviewer's eyes. The best way to do both is get an external camera and move the onscreen picture of the interviewer right below it.

As a career coach, it's important that you model what you're teaching. You'll lose credibility if you're trying to teach someone how to look professional for Zoom and all you do is open your laptop to take a call. Follow the above steps yourself before you walk a client through them, and make sure you own environment is Zoom-ready.

## TOP QUESTIONS TO NAIL

Here's where we pull together all of our storytelling, charisma, and executive presence tools to help your clients craft engaging answers to the interview questions they're most likely to get asked.

**Tell me about yourself.**

Not all interviews include this, but when they do, it's always the very first question out of the gate. That means the answer is the first impression your client will make on the interviewer. Note: this question might sound more like "Walk me through your résumé" or "Walk me through your background."

Coach your client to give a three-part answer. Humans like and respond well to things given in groups of three. Here your client should break down their answer into 1) the moment they knew they were meant to do this work; 2) gratitude leading into a chronology ("and I've been so lucky I've been able to do that ever since …"); and 3) a simple summarizing statement that lets the interview know you're about to stop talking so there's no awkward silence and the interview feels more like a conversation. A solid example is: "So that's a little bit about me."

**Why are you looking for a new role?**

Alternatively: "Why are you leaving?" or "Why are you considering another opportunity?" If your client has already left their previous position, this question might instead be why they left.

Here it's best to answer in a way that puts the emphasis on moving toward something as opposed to running away. Encourage your client to answer honestly, and to emphasize that there's something really intriguing about the opportunity in front of them.

Whatever your client says, urge them to keep it short. The longer it takes to answer this question, the more recruiters wonder about the *real* story of why you've left.

**Tell me about your _______ experience.**

If this were my job interview, it would be "Tell me about your human resources leadership experience." Instead it will be about whatever your client's background is.

This is *another place* where the "strategic, three-story" answer comes into play. This will help your client step back and give the interviewer a 10,000-foot overview of their experience. If I were answering this question, I'd say something like, "I have twenty years of human resources experience. I've led human resources teams in three different industries: finance, manufacturing, and healthcare. I've led teams that are all in one location and teams that are scattered all across the United States. The largest area of responsibility has been 15,000 employees under my organization. I've also led teams where, as a VP, I led directors who had managers and such." In one strategic statement, you get a nice overview of all of my experience.

Then I dive into my experience today, which I would chunk into three because we sound like leaders when we speak in threes: "My three main responsibilities in human resources leadership have always been, one, cultural integration, two, talent acquisition, and three, executive coaching."

That's it. Just clump it into threes.

Then your clients should tell a story: "The most interesting initiative I worked on recently was when I helped our organization identify our cultural values," etc.

Teach your client this structure, and then when they get thrown a question like "Describe this experience," they can organize a lot of information in this format and sound cogent.

## What are you doing now?

This is probably the most frequently asked question. It might sound like "Tell me about your most recent role" if they've left that job.

You would want to capture the information that makes up this answer and help your client put it into that "Strategic Three Story" framework so that the interviewer hears the overall organization and how they fit into it. That means talking about their three main initiatives, achievements, or areas of responsibility, followed by a story.

## Why do you want to work here?

The interviewer wants to know what your client knows about the company. They might say, "What do you know about us?" instead.

However it's asked, I recommend the same answer, broken down into two categories. The first is a list of what your client knows about the organization. This is like a Wikipedia entry. You want the interviewer to think, "Oh, they've done their homework."

The second part is for your client to name one thing about the company that they're in love with. Not something that's really about your client ("I love your company culture, and I really want to work in it!") but truly and seriously only about the company. This should land for the interviewer just the way it might when someone says, "You have the most beautiful eyes." They should feel that their company is seen and appreciated.

## What is your greatest strength?

This might be asked as "What sets you apart?"

You can help your client most by really digging into their greatest strength long before they find themselves in an interview. This may be hard for them to articulate because our greatest strengths are the things that seem easy. They flow from us. There's no friction, like there is with our weaknesses, which most of us confront every single day.

This is a good conversation to have with a client, to get down to the essence of their greatest strength. It should always be their strength as it evidences itself in both their personal life and professional life. Don't pick a strength that's based solely upon their job.

Discourage your client from giving bland answers like "My greatest strength is leading people." Everyone says that, and they all sound the same to the interviewer. When your client answers from who they really are and shares their unique greatest strength, the interviewer thinks, "You really know yourself. You're quite self-aware."

Hint: the client's greatest strength is often the flip side of their greatest weakness. So if they're stumped for a strength, start there.

Taylor is an ideal example. He's always been fascinated by the world of ideas, and his brain goes a mile a minute. This was hard on his parents when he was a kid because he was always talking: asking questions, rattling off hypothetical answers, proposing off-the-wall theories and concepts. "My parents were, like, shut up," he tells me.

But Taylor's greatest weakness—his intense curiosity and motor mouth—is also his superpower. "I'm an idea machine," he says. "I love ideas—mine or somebody else's, it doesn't matter. I love combining ideas in service of really big things. My greatest joy is when people add something to the conversation."

A three-week behavioral camp in Hawaii led Taylor to his passion. He met other kids like him, kids who were into STEM subjects like oceanography. "The most minute thing is a molecule," Taylor says. "Everything is a molecule."

Today, Taylor is a molecular scientist. And his ideas are very, very welcome.

**What is your greatest weakness?**

Tell your client to say something real, not overused answers like "I'm a workaholic" or "I'm a perfectionist." Coach them to talk about the number one thing that has really held them back. Whatever answer they use, it should be far shorter than their answer about their greatest strength.

They could say it this way: "My greatest weakness is I can't stand hierarchy. It's very difficult for me to work in a very hierarchal structure because I know this about myself—"

Note the second component of this answer. "Because I know this about myself." That's important. Here your client might say, "I need to remind myself to be respectful and not just barge into people's offices, which could be off-putting to some people."

Then the third thing they should tack on is, "I know I'll always have to deal with this."

Help your client understand that they should always divulge their real, genuine weakness. Because we hiring managers see it. We do. If your client says something that isn't quite on target, then we'll think they're not self-aware or they're not confident enough to share what their real weakness is. Both of those are red flags.

## Tell me about a time when you …

The answer a hiring manager is looking for here is about your client's behaviors of success. They believe that if people show successful behaviors today and in the past, it's a reliable predictor of successful behaviors in the future. The best way to answer behavior-based interview questions is by using the SOAR method. Situation, Obstacle, Action, and Result. Tell a story that covers all four points.

Let's have a little fun with this. Say that the behavior-based question from the interviewer is: "Tell me about a time when you had to defend your belief that pineapple is great on pizza."

Using the SOAR method, you might say: "I was at a pizza joint with some friends, and I wanted pineapple on the pizza we were ordering. No one else did, even though most of them admitted they'd never tried it. So I offered to buy a small pizza just for me with pineapple and ham, and told them that if anyone who tried a bite liked it, I'd personally buy a larger pizza with the same for the table. Out of six people, four of them ended up loving my topping combination. I was out another $15, but I got the pizza I wanted, and I converted my friends to fans for future pizza fun."

## What is your philosophy around diversity, equity, and inclusion?

This is a question we're seeing much more often. Borders are really falling and our ability to work across cultural lines is becoming more and more important. My recommendation is to work with your client and come up with really deep, thoughtful answers.

Taylor is a good example here. When I ask him about his take on DEI, he was initially uncomfortable. "I'm an old white man," he says. "What would I have to say about that?"

So I ask him if there was anything that had ever happened in his life that helped him understand privilege and the lack of it.

Immediately, Taylor has an answer. Taylor was a problem kid, frequently sent to the principal's office for his inability to keep his mouth shut in class. At the behavioral camp he attended in Hawaii (which, incidentally, was for troubled youth), he was thrown in with the truly hardcore underprivileged. The camp was run by the University of Hawaii Hilo marine biology department as a means to reversing Hawaii's alarming high school dropout rate, and Taylor was surrounded by brown kids with troubled childhoods but a passion, like his, for ideas and science. "I had the chance to go on to get a degree in molecular biology," he says. "How many of them did?"

After Taylor graduated, he worked in Germany, where he was seen as "other" and even unwelcome. "I was American. I was different. I was sweaty," he says. "I was everything the Germans didn't like. I looked like them, but I was not them. And they made sure I knew it." He got a lesson in being excluded.

On another job, in Brazil, he was also different—but there he was warmly accepted and welcomed in local homes. These disparate experiences ignited something in him and fueled his innate curiosity to think about the differences—and similarities—between people.

Any of these stories are a much better answer than "I'm just an old white man."

**(Mic drop)**

This isn't a question or an answer. It's what happens at the end of the interviewer's questions for your client. This is where your client says something like, "Oh wait, before we hang up, I just want to say thank you so much for taking this time. When I knew we were going to be meeting today, I had some sleepless nights, in a good way because I was so excited to be able to talk with you. I so appreciate your time, energy, and all the information that you shared. I know you have a lot of candidates. Of course, I would love to be the person to move to the next step, but I trust your process. I just want to say thank you. Thank you so much." Pure gratitude, no sell. Mic drop.

Finally, help your client come up with prepared questions so that when they're asked, "What questions do you have for me?" they have a list. The best question is based on something the interviewer said: "You recently mentioned this," or "I've read this," or "The person I met yesterday said this."

Tell your client not to go online to research the best questions. Everyone does it, and that makes everyone sound alike.

When I'm prepping clients for interviews, I always ask them what questions they're concerned about or aren't sure they have the right answers to. I ask them to hand-write their answers, edit them down, and integrate storytelling, so they feel confident when they walk into an interview.

# CHAPTER TEN

# The Magic of the Completed Circle

Benny is in trouble. We've been working together for six months, and he finally lands a job as an executive director for a nonprofit in Virginia. This is an important role for him because he was out of work for over two years. But less than nine months after he starts his new job, I get a voicemail from him.

"Hey Cara, it's Benny. I think I'm going to get fired. Can you help me get another job?"

The two years he spent searching before landing this job are still messing with his head. The board chair of his new company, Candace, reminds him too much of his old boss, the one who'd fired him before his long dry spell. Benny's only been in place a few months, but he's already starting to slide. Now I'm reading his Performance Improvement Plan that Candace delivered to him last week. He has thirty days to improve or he's out.

"Benny, do you want to leave?" I ask.

"I'm afraid that if I do leave, it'll take me another two and a half years to find another job."

Together we agree to work intensely to try to save his current job. Even though he's nine months in, he needs to go back to basics. He needs to approach it as if he's starting at a new job.

We implement the First Ninety Days activities. Candace responds positively. Benny now begins to outline strategies. Candace decides to extend his thirty-day probation, since she's seeing progress. We then execute a plan that ends the year with a removal of the Performance Improvement Plan and a raise.

It's a lot of hard work and reading between the lines and tea leaves to help Benny navigate the dynamics of the relationships he has with Candace, the rest of the board, and his team. And the most important dynamic: his relationship with his own mind. It also confirms for me that the First Ninety Days are critical. Imperative.

It can also be implemented well after the client has started in their role.

## THE FIRST NINETY DAYS

Congratulations! Your client landed the job! It's a big, big deal. And: your work is far from over.

Your client wants to live happily ever after. You want them to live happily ever after. But they just came through a career change, one of the top ten life stressors, and now they're making their way in a new world. What if you could help them manage the first ninety days after the hire to make sure they start their new role on solid footing? What if you knew that what you do in this first ninety days could result in your client's new boss saying to them, "You're one of the best hires I've ever made"? That's what my clients have heard—more than once. I know it's a direct result of the First Ninety Days onboarding process I coach them through, based on Michael Watkin's book of the same name.

The First Ninety Days process has four phases, the duration of which is dependent on the complexity and pace of the company, the client's role, and the company's requirements for results. Each phase represents a shift in energy and focus from your client.

**Phase 1: Define**

This phase starts just before the first day, and it's the most important part of onboarding. That's because this is when your client should be asking questions and getting clear on the expectations for their role. Ironically this is often when new hires go quiet. They're afraid they're supposed to know those expectations already. They worry that it's a little late to start asking for clarification.

The reality is that any organization knows new hires take time to get up to speed. From that perspective asking questions is not only welcome but preferable to someone just jumping in and screwing up because they don't know the lay of the land. This is absolutely the right time for your client to ask questions and get a handle on defining expectations.

So encourage them to do so. Even before day one, coach your client to review the notes they took during their interview process (don't worry, they took notes—you coached them to do so). They should also reread the original job posting and description. Then ask them to write out their vision of their role based on what they know so far.

The next step, not long after they're on the job, is for them to sit with their supervisor or leader and refine that vision by asking defining questions like:

- What are the top problems I'm here to solve?
- What tools do I need?
- What do I need to know before I start?
- Who are my key stakeholders?
- How is success measured?
- What behaviors are rewarded in this culture?
- What behaviors are frowned upon in this culture?

Your client should take note of people to meet, training classes to take, meetings to attend, and product information to review. All of this—the answers to the questions above and anything else they learn—should be used to create a final vision statement for their role that identifies the overarching problem to solve and the overarching project or task intended to do so.

Obviously that overarching project will be made up of many smaller ones. During their first month, your client will outline three to five sub-projects that emerge from their conversations with others in the organization. Each project should be well-defined, with key performance indicators that are SMART, specific, measured, achievable, relevant, and time-bound. They should identify any milestones or evidence of progress.

Of course it's key that your client set up regular meetings with their leader—at least once a week for the first month. During those meetings your client should review their role's vision statement with an emphasis on it being a work in progress, so their leader can move things around and provide clarity on what needs to be done. This is all part of your client getting their leader's buy-in on what they're working on, what success looks like, and what tools are needed to get those projects done.

## Phase 2: Learn

Starting around day thirty, this is when your client begins to get a firm grasp of the culture, cadence, people, and structure of the organization. They'll learn this about ten percent of the time through structured learning, twenty percent of the time through coaching or mentorship, and the balance through doing—usually a challenging project.

We think of structured learning as the most important when in actuality we spend the least time on it. Most of your client's on-the-job learning will take place while they're tackling the projects identified in the define phase.

That learning comes through welcome meetings with key stakeholders, peers, and team members; a culture overview of the organization including pitfalls; getting clear on tech needs like laptop, mobile apps, and tech training; getting used to the pace of 1:1 meetings, team meetings, and all-hands meetings; and work groups, project reviews, and discussions.

It's a lot. Your client will likely feel overwhelmed, so advise them to take lots of notes and keep their thoughts well organized.

## Phase 3: Build

This phase begins around day sixty. This is when relationships solidify and trust gets established. Social ties can also result in early wins, so your client should focus on strategy execution through relationships and spend extra time listening carefully and meeting commitments.

By now the document that started with their role's vision statement and three to five projects is probably multiple pages. Coach your client to create a one–page summary—a dashboard or scorecard to keep track of current project status and progress.

## Phase 4: Do

Beginning around day ninety, this is when a new hire shifts into full execution mode and not before. To do so earlier than this is inadvisable; most new employees will not have absorbed enough information and established enough relationships to create a sound strategy.

Consider changing the frequency of your meetings with your client in this phase. Help them celebrate all the wins and evaluate their progress during this period of execution.

## The First Ninety Days: Not Just for New Hires

Madhu is a boomerang client. I help her land a job at one of the Alphabet companies of Google, and now she is ready for a promotion. The problem is that she works for someone who's quite new to her, since her boss and her bosses' boss—her advocates and the people who brought her into the company in the first place—are gone.

We go back to the First Ninety Days and implement many of the same activities so that she's in close alignment with her new boss. Today Madhu is up for a nice promotion.

## THE COMPLETION CALL

Depending on whether or not I take a client through the First Ninety Days process, the hire can be where my client engagement ends—for the time being.

This transition is a beautiful, magical way to say "so long for now" as you and your client go your separate ways on your own journeys. While it feels like coming full circle with your coaching, it's actually more like a spiral: look down its length, and you'll see that you are actually still moving forward.

The completion call symbolizes the end of this part of your client's career journey. It is on this call that you'll answer any lingering questions they may have, and then discuss three questions:

1. Looking back on our time together, what's the one thing you've realized you'd like to start doing?
2. What's the one thing you've realized you want to stop doing?
3. What's the one thing you've realized that you're actually very good at and you want to continue to do?

Start, stop, continue. It's a wonderful moment of self-reflection that crystallizes for your client the most helpful points of the coaching relationship and anchors your relationship with them.

## COMING TO YOUR COMPLETION

And with that, we've come "full circle" (remember, it's actually a forward spiral) in your learning as well. The remaining chapter will cover advanced magic and stands a bit outside the rest of your learning, and so I leave you here with three questions in our journey together:

1. What's one thing you've learned about yourself through reading this book that you will start doing?
2. What's one thing you're going to stop doing (that is not the opposite of the previous question)?
3. And what's one thing you've realized you're actually quite good at that you will continue to do?

# CHAPTER ELEVEN

# Advanced Magic for Special Situations

I don't know until the very end of our career coach certification class that the day Amy signed up was one of the lowest points in her life. She'd been in a toxic work situation and had been let go in a very disheartening way. She was reeling from the uncertainty of it all and at the end of her rope.

"This program was a breath of fresh air to me," she tells me. "I don't know if you knew that. It gave me hope."

While Amy trains to be a career coach, she takes a new job she doesn't like but that gives her and her husband health benefits. "I see them as just another client who pays for different things for my business," she says, and I can hear that this reframe helps her stay motivated. But as we end our call, I'm certain she will never launch her business. I know because a little voice inside my head, that little bit of magic that tells me things I couldn't possibly know, whispers, "Amy will continue to dream, and only dream, of what could be."

This chapter is the best of all the magic I can impart to you. It's what you need to overcome the biggest obstacle of them all: busyness.

## BUSYNESS IS BS

Busyness is the biggest thing that sabotages people starting their own thriving coaching business. We humans are like that. We do all sorts of things that get in the way of getting what we want.

What do you want? I'm guessing that you'd like to make a really big impact by helping people. You picture seeing someone's face light up as you help them figure out what they're meant to do in this world. You know that when you get that call from your client telling you they got the job, it will be an amazing feeling, a feeling as close to undiluted happiness as you can imagine.

And for some reason, you'll think you're moving closer to launching your own career coaching practice when all you're doing is staying busy.

You start researching company names.

You see if your name has a URL.

You identify what you need to do to DBA your new company name.

You sign up for a free wix.com site and start building your website.

You decide that you want to write a book.

You sign up for another certification course.

You decide to take a marketing course online.

You find out if your DISC is the same and take another assessment and then realize that you've always wanted to become a Gallup StrengthsFinder assessor and sign up for a class.

You research becoming ICF ACC certified.

You spend three days researching someone to create your logo for you.

You design your new business card and then decide that you want to use moo.com instead.

You think you're moving forward, but all you're doing is being busy. And none of this busy work will get you to your dream of starting your own career coaching business.

That is what you need to do:

Stop preparing for your business. Open your business.

## ELIXIR TO CURE WHATABOUTISM

But what about my program? But what about my pricing? But what if they ask me a question I don't know? But what if I don't get any leads? But what about digital marketing?

I have the perfect cure-all for your whataboutisms. *Launch your business and get your first client.* That is when everything will become clear.

Lori had been a vice president of a large athletic wear company with a certification under her belt as a college counselor. She takes our career coach certification course and joins the Path, our alumni group where we continue to offer our career coaches support. She is about to sign up for a life coaching program in the San Rafael area of northern California when I tell her to stop. "There isn't anything more you need to learn to be an amazing career coach, Lori."

"But, but, but …" Lori stutters. "But I don't have an MBA like you do. I don't have twenty years of human resources and recruiting experience. I haven't written a book. I don't have a fraction of your credentials. And you think I'm ready?"

I assure her that I do, and she is.

Not long after, I read a message from Lori on our collaboration platform: "Help! I got a client, and they asked me how to pay me, anyone know how to set up a virtual terminal?"

Lori figures it out. Of course she does. Landing her first real paying client forces her to build things days before the initial client meeting. In two months, Lori has her entire program built and is on her way to onboarding a second client. This time the payment goes much more smoothly. By the time Lori reaches the end of her third month after graduation, she posts this in our platform:

"I made $10,000 this month."

Click.

It is in this moment that I know it finally clicks for Lori. She has her own viable career coaching business. I also know she never would have gotten to this point by taking another class or working on her website (which she never created and still hasn't). It could only happen with the launch of her business.

Now Lori teaches more junior career coaches in our Path community, and I hear her say, "I used to be so nervous, and I understand. You'll get there, trust me."

## FACING OUR NERVES

My son Eric has a job interview—and a big problem. It's with a law firm in Santa Barbara, and his suit is thousands of miles away. I think about jumping in the car, driving six hours down, dropping off his suit, and driving back up, but it simply isn't an option for me. Then Eric says, "Don't worry, Mom. I've got this."

On the day of his interview, he tells me, he arrives forty-five minutes early and just sits there in the waiting room with the receptionist smiling at his enthusiastic naivete.

"But what did you do about a suit?" I ask.

"I stood next to guys at my dorm and when someone was about my size, I asked him, 'Hey, got a suit?'" He tells me. "And then I put my foot next to other guys and asked, 'Got dress shoes?'"

He goes on to say, "I was so nervous, but I learned so much."

It dawns on me at that moment that I haven't felt those kinds of nerves in a very long time. In fact I've done a lot throughout the years to avoid feeling like that. I tell my son, "Eric, remember this feeling because over the years you'll feel less and less of it. But put yourself in situations where you feel it again. It might be in those moments that you really grow."

The best magic I know for facing down your nerves and your fear is to welcome in those feelings. Cherish the moments. Put yourself in situations where you're doing something so utterly uncomfortable that you can't help but grow.

Claim to be a lifelong learner? Prove it to yourself. Stop being busy. Do the things.

A new client remarked that once she *claimed* her new career path, things seemed to magically open up for her. A longtime operations leader posted on her LinkedIn that she's pursuing a passion and career in diversity, equity, and inclusion. All of a sudden, applications that have been sitting have suddenly caught the attention of recruiters. Now she has several interviews lined up.

I've also seen the opposite.

One longtime client reached back out to me three years after he'd discovered what he really wanted to do in life, but had been too concerned to take a step forward. Since our engagement, he's lost two jobs and is facing yet another layoff. On the phone, he sighed, "Do you think the universe is trying to tell me something?"

These client stories remind me of other stories I've read about how when people take a step in a direction, sometimes a very radical direction divergent from their current path, things suddenly open up for them.

I think about a neighborhood magic shop that a young man named James Doty visited on the day he lost one of his fingers. How he let his curiosity move his feet. The tinkling of the store's doorbell, which brought the owner out to talk with him. Today James is Dr. Doty and author of *Into the Magic Shop: A Neurosurgeon's Quest to Discover the Mysteries of the Brain and the Secrets of the Heart.*

I think about USAF and US Navy Seal David Goggins, who signed up for a running competition he needed in order to qualify to run in the biggest Badwater Ultramarathon and fundraise for his fellow soldiers' families. Even though he had zero running training, Goggins completed the 24-hour ultramarathon, proving that the strongest part of his body is his mind. He tells his story in his memoir *Can't Hurt Me: Master Your Mind and Defy the Odds.*

I think about Spanx founder Sara Blakely who, early on, went to Macy's and dragged the display of her company's undergarments next to the register so they'd start selling. It led to her appearing on *Oprah*, after which everything took off.

Sharp right turns. All because something changed, because these people felt deep in their gut that they knew what they had to do.

It's a validation of something I've recently come to know: Remarkable things happen when we let our hearts lead our steps. When we quiet the mind and let our soul reach out, magical things transpire. Things we've never imagined come about.

These things bring a tinge of fear and a lot of excitement. Like standing at the top of a waterfall thirty feet up in the air with all of your friends who've already made the dive swimming way down below in the blue and yelling, "Jump, Cara!"

Starting my own business was very much like that. And you know what? It still is. Every month brings something new. A challenge. A failure. A success. A small pathway I didn't see before that is now revealed. That same curiosity takes over, and I take a small step forward, wondering where this path will lead me.

I've shared my journey with you and how this business came to be. Teaching you how to lay a solid foundation from your niche so you coach the people who ignite your soul. How to coach your clients to find their true north. How to create a beautiful, engaging narrative of your client's experience in the dossier. How to execute go-to-market strategies that get your clients seen so they can get on with their careers.

We've discussed how everyone can become more confident, magnetic, and charismatic—that these are skills we can learn, not something we're born knowing. We've talked about how to bring your clients full circle in their engagement with you so that they leave feeling complete and ready to tackle one of the top searches of their lives: their job. And I've shared several tricks to help you overcome your own fears of launching your career coaching business so *you* can feel complete and ready to do what you know in your heart you're meant to do: help people.

Now you know the small steps you can take with confidence, and that as you build your own resilience, you, in turn, help others build theirs. These are tangible items on a checklist, yes, but they're infused with woo-woo stuff that you might have come to realize appeals to you while you've been reading this book.

There is something bigger brewing in your spirit, something bubbling, something growing, something newly seen. You've felt this feeling before, long ago. Maybe you even squashed it because its intensity scared you.

I think of a book title I saw long ago: *Guts & Borrowed Money: Straight Talk for Starting and Growing Your Small Business.* Yes, we need both bravery and capital. But entrepreneurs also need, I think, a deep, insatiable curiosity. You've got that. That's why you're here, finishing this book.

The humdrum life of the corporate office, where the cleaning crew comes and empties your recycling bins each night, is just too regular, too predictable for you. You get bored after a while, and you try to poke the bear for more work or a wider range of activities. No one is interested in you changing or growing. Thwarted, you sit staring out your office window, thinking there must be something more to life than this.

If you let yourself sit for a minute in a quiet spot, you just might feel something shift. A slight change of pressure in the room. Turning, you might see a door appear out of thin air, one that ignites a long-dormant flame.

You stand, reach for the knob, and open the door to the possibility of doing more, for more. Of leveraging all of your skills, talents, and hidden gifts. Being fully expressed.

Something builds in your soul. It's that excitement again. The joy of learning something new and creating something out of nothing. Yes, it's scary—the good kind of scary. And you wonder, "Should I walk through?"

I'm here to encourage you to walk through.

And when you do, I'll see you on the other side.

If you want to learn more about becoming a certified career coach, tapping into your magic, and making a positive impact in this world, reach out to me at www.iacareercoaches.org.

# ACKNOWLEDGMENTS

This book was meant to replace my second book: *Confessions of the Accidental Career Coach*. A second edition of sorts. But as time went on and changes came to the industry, it evolved into a stand-alone guide for a different kind of reader: seasoned career coaches wanting to take their practices to the next level. So this book became number three, and it was harder than I thought it would be. Even though by now I'm more accustomed to the process of creating and publishing a book, I really wanted this one to be the best ... because it might possibly be my last. Because of that, I'd like to thank the individuals who were instrumental in birthing this book into the world.

None of my books would have been possible without the love and support of my husband, Edgar Heilmann. He continues to be my number one advocate and supporter, ever encouraging me to take the time needed to do what I need to do. He has stood by my side for coming up to thirty years, through the happiest moments of my life and through every deep struggle. Edgar, you are my best friend and my true love, and I thank you, the keeper of my heart.

I am forever grateful to my two sons, Eric and Andrew, constant sources of hilarious "first interview" stories that hold everlasting lessons of leaning in, raising hands, and taking the most uncomfortable steps to getting their first jobs. Through my young adult children's lives, I experience what it is like again to really want a job and be so utterly disappointed when the rejection email arrives. And the feeling of pride, relief, and new anxiety when an offer arrives.

To my early boss at the University of Hawaii Bookstore: you forgot it was my first day, had me only clean bookshelves all day, and were startled to find me still cleaning them at the end of the day because you'd forgotten I was there. Thank you. To my last boss, who thought being a boss was having employees in hopes that would they lead themselves, I thank you. These bookend experiences encouraged me to strike out on my own. If life in corporate America had been better for me, none of this would have existed. Thank you for reminding me that in the ecosystems of your world, I wasn't important enough to integrate and that I needed to build my own ecosystem where all of those parts of me and those around me know that they are utterly important and belong.

And through these entrepreneurial ups and downs amidst a pandemic and beyond, a very special thanks goes to my author mastermind group with Aicha Bascaro, Amari Ice, Meredith Holley, and Tami Stackelhouse. And our OG leader, Angela Lauria, our publisher and business coach. You are the tallest tree in our forest, and through your deep roots, we have formed our own forests and continue to nurture one another.

To every single career coach who has a voice, a struggle, a fear: your doubts are motivating and inspiring. None of this comes easy, but you do it all because of your love for your clients. The joy when one of your clients says they got a job offer. The excitement when your client gets the promotion. The happiness when someone out of the workforce for ten years lands the job of their dreams. To you, leaders at the International Association of Career Coaches, Michelle Traino, Ruth Vitzkovitz, Annette Garsteck, Olesia Iakivchyk, Jo Abbott, Sonia Jackson, Nicole Croizier, and Christy Watz—and other brave coaches who voiced your struggles—the soul of this book is for you. Thank you for your transparency; now we don't feel alone and know that together we can make it happen.

And to those who have been a part of getting me there: Michelle Hoffmann, Lisa Virtue, Andrew Sloss, Nurys Harrigan-Pedersen, and Dr. Michael Kennedy. And Dr. James R. Doty, whom I asked to be part of my early reader group because of his book, *Into the Magic Shop: A Neurosurgeon's Quest to Discover the Mysteries of the Brain and the Secrets of the Heart*—your book inspired me to write what I know to be true, that there is magic in this world. A shout out to Ninon Shesgreen with her special gift of making the external world beautiful so I can have a sacred space to do my craft. And to Amy Glynn, for being my literary urban dictionary and fellow wordy.

And finally, to Maggie Reynolds, my muse: I loved it when you edited my first book, *The Art of Finding the Job You Love*. I loved your style and encouraging words as I struggled through the editing process. And I am so thankful that we've reconnected, reunited, for this third and possibly final business book. I honestly don't know how I could have done it without you. You have a gift for words and a honed craft that has made this process truly a joy. Thank you for sharing so much about yourself, your journey, the journey of your other authors, and weird anecdotal moments of serendipity that made it crystal clear that we were meant to work on this book together.

Thank you all for being part of this incredible journey.

For the past twenty years, Cara has helped people get jobs. But not just any jobs, jobs they love. A former Chief Talent Officer and Human Resources executive for large national and international companies including ARAMARK, Kaiser Permanente, and AMN Healthcare, she now trains future career coaches to build successful businesses so they can help people get jobs they love.

Cara is President of the International Association of Career Coaches (IACC)®, a global consortium of professional career coaches, and founder of Ready Reset Go®. She is a recognized expert and has been featured in *Forbes* and *The Wall Street Journal*. Cara is a best-selling author of three books: *The Art of Finding the Job You Love*, *Confessions of the Accidental Career Coach*, and *Ready, Set, Go!*, co-authored with world-renowned author and speaker Brian Tracy.

Cara holds an MBA from Vanderbilt University's Owen School of Management and a Bachelor of Business from the

University of Hawaii. She is a certified Senior Professional in Human Resources, a Certified Professional Résumé Writer, a Senior Professional Career Coach, a Master Professional Career Coach, and a member of the invitation-only FORBES® Coaches Council.

She is an avid community volunteer who has served on the Board of Wardrobe for Opportunity, a nonprofit in Oakland dedicated to ending poverty by helping individuals get a job, keep a job, and build a career. Cara and her husband reside in the San Francisco Bay Area, where she loves hiking and running through the East Bay hills.

Cara loves to hear from people. Feel free to connect:

www.linkedin.com/in/caraheilmann/
www.iacareercoaches.org
www.readyresetgo.com
@CaraHeilmann
cara@iacareercoaches.org